THE 100 MOST IMPORTANT BIBLE VERSES EVERY WOMAN MUST KNOW!

SMITH
FREEMAN
Publishing

CONTENTS

A Message to Readers

God has given us a book of promises upon which we, as Christians, can and must depend. The Bible is a priceless gift, a tool that God intends for us to use in every aspect of our lives. Too many Christians, however, keep their spiritual tool kits tightly closed and out of sight, sometimes with tragic consequences.

How desperately our world needs strong Christian women who are willing to honor God with their praise and their service. This generation faces problems that defy easy solutions, yet face them we must. So we need courageous believers who are willing to read God's Word, to trust it, and to act upon it.

This book contains one hundred Bible verses that every Christian woman, including you, should know by heart. In fact, these verses contain some of the most important truths you'll ever learn. So, it's no wonder that the ideas on these pages can provide wisdom, courage, and energy for your daily journey.

Are you tired? Discouraged? Fearful? Be comforted and trust the promises that God has made to you.

Are you worried or anxious? Be confident in God's power. He will never desert you.

Do you see a difficult future ahead? Be courageous and call upon the Lord. He will protect you and then use you according to His purposes.

Are you confused? Listen to the quiet voice of your heavenly Father. He is not a God of confusion. Talk with Him; listen to Him; trust Him, and trust His promises. He is steadfast, and He is your Protector . . . now and forever.

1

ABUNDANCE

I have come that they may have life,
and that they may have it more abundantly.
JOHN 10:10 NKJV

God's abundance is available to each of us. He offers His blessings, but He doesn't force them upon us. To receive them, we must trust His promises and follow, as closely as we can, in the footsteps of His Son. But the world tempts us to do otherwise.

Everywhere you turn, someone or something is vying for your attention, trying to convince you that peace and happiness are commodities that can be purchased for the right price. But, buyer beware. Genuine peace and spiritual abundance are not for sale at any price. Real abundance is never obtained through worldly possessions. It results from your relationship with God.

Are you a woman who seeks the abundant life that Jesus promises in John 10:10? Then turn your life and your heart over to Him. When you do, you'll receive the love, the peace, and the abundance that can only come from the touch of the Master's hand.

*Knowing that your future is absolutely assured
can free you to live abundantly today.*
SARAH YOUNG

*God is the giver, and we are the receivers.
And His richest gifts are bestowed not upon those
who do the greatest things, but upon those who
accept His abundance and His grace.*
HANNAH WHITALL SMITH

*The gift of God is eternal life, spiritual life,
abundant life through faith in Jesus Christ,
the Living Word of God.*
ANNE GRAHAM LOTZ

*God's riches are beyond anything we could ask
or even dare to imagine! If my life gets gooey and stale,
I have no excuse.*
BARBARA JOHNSON

*Get ready for God to show you not only His pleasure,
but His approval.*
JONI EARECKSON TADA

More from God's Word

Until now you have asked for nothing in My name.
Ask and you will receive, that your joy may be complete.
John 16:24 HCSB

Success, success to you, and success to those who help you,
for your God will help you.
1 Chronicles 12:18 NIV

And God is able to make all grace abound to you,
so that always having all sufficiency in everything,
you may have an abundance for every good deed.
2 Corinthians 9:8 NASB

My cup runs over. Surely goodness and mercy
shall follow me all the days of my life;
and I will dwell in the house of the Lord forever.
Psalm 23:5-6 NKJV

The Lord bless you and keep you; the Lord make
His face shine upon you, and be gracious to you.
Numbers 6:24–25 NKJV

A Timely Tip

God wants you to experience the kind of spiritual abundance that only He can provide. When you stay focused on His will, He will provide for your needs.

2

ACCEPTANCE

*Should we accept only good things from the hand of God
and never anything bad?*

JOB 2:10 NLT

Manmade plans are fallible; God's plans are not. Yet whenever life takes an unexpected turn, we are tempted to fall into the spiritual traps of worry, self-pity, or bitterness. God intends that we do otherwise.

The old saying is familiar: "Forgive and forget." But when we have been hurt badly, forgiveness is often difficult, and forgetting is downright impossible. Since we can't forget yesterday's troubles, we should learn from them. Yesterday has much to teach us about tomorrow. We may learn from the past, but we should never live in the past. God has given each of us a glorious day: this one. And it's up to each of us to use this day as faithful stewards, not as embittered historians.

So if you're trying to forget the past, don't waste your time. Instead, try a different approach: learn to accept the past and live in the present. Then you can focus your thoughts and your energies, not on the struggles of yesterday, but instead on the profound opportunities that God has placed before you today.

Accept each day as it comes to you. Do not waste your time and energy wishing for a different set of circumstances.
SARAH YOUNG

It is always possible to do the will of God. In every place and time it is within our power to acquiesce in the will of God.
ELISABETH ELLIOT

When we face an impossible situation, all self-reliance and self-confidence must melt away; we must be totally dependent on Him for the resources.
ANNE GRAHAM LOTZ

We must meet our disappointments, our persecutions, our malicious enemies, our provoking friends, our trials and temptations of every sort, with an attitude of surrender and trust. We must spread our wings and "mount up" to the "heavenly places in Christ" above them all, where they will lose their power to harm or distress us.
HANNAH WHITALL SMITH

Don't waste energy regretting the way things are or thinking about what might have been. Start at the present moment— accepting things exactly as they are—and search for My way in the midst of those circumstances.
SARAH YOUNG

More from God's Word

Everything God made is good, and nothing should
be refused if it is accepted with thanks.
1 Timothy 4:4 NCV

Trust in the Lord with all your heart
and lean not on your own understanding....
Proverbs 3:5 NIV

He is the Lord. He will do what He thinks is good.
1 Samuel 3:18 HCSB

For the Yahweh is good, and His love is eternal;
His faithfulness endures through all generations.
Psalm 100:5 HCSB

For now we see in a mirror, dimly,
but then face to face. Now I know in part,
but then I shall know just as I also am known.
1 Corinthians 13:12 NKJV

A Timely Tip

Whenever you encounter situations that you cannot change, you must learn the wisdom of acceptance. And you must learn to trust God.

3

ACCEPTING CHRIST

*For God so loved the world, that he gave his
only begotten Son, that whosoever believeth in him
should not perish, but have everlasting life.*

JOHN 3:16 KJV

Jesus came to this world in order that each of us might live abundantly and eternally. He came so that our joy might be complete here on earth and, more importantly, in heaven. Christ loved us so much that He endured unspeakable pain on the cross so that we might be with Him throughout eternity.

How will you respond to Christ's sacrifice? Will you give Him your heart, your mind, and your soul? And will you accept the gift of eternal life, a gift that cost Him so much but can be yours for the asking? It's the most important decision you'll ever make. And if you choose wisely, it's a decision that you'll never regret.

Ultimately, our relationship with Christ
is the one thing we cannot do without.
BETH MOORE

The crucial question for each of us is this:
What do you think of Jesus, and do you yet have
a personal acquaintance with Him?
HANNAH WHITALL SMITH

Blessed assurance, Jesus is mine!
O what a foretaste of glory divine!
FANNY CROSBY

Trust God's Word and His power more than you trust
your own feelings and experiences. Remember,
your Rock is Christ, and it is the sea
that ebbs and flows with the tides, not Him.
LETTIE COWMAN

Christ is the horn of our salvation,
the One who was secured on a cross
so that we could be secured in the Lamb's book of Life.
BETH MOORE

More from God's Word

And this is the testimony: God has given us eternal life,
and this life is in His Son. The one who has the Son has life.
The one who doesn't have the Son of God does not have life.
1 JOHN 5:11–12 HCSB

The Spirit of God, who raised Jesus from the dead, lives in you.
And just as he raised Christ from the dead, he will give life
to your mortal bodies by this same Spirit living within you.
ROMANS 8:11 NLT

For the wages of sin is death, but the gift of God
is eternal life in Christ Jesus our Lord.
ROMANS 6:23 NIV

Therefore we were buried with Him by baptism into death,
in order that, just as Christ was raised from the dead by the
glory of the Father, so we too may walk in a new way of life.
ROMANS 6:4 HCSB

I am the good shepherd.
The good shepherd lays down his life for the sheep.
JOHN 10:11 NIV

A Timely Tip

The ultimate choice, the most important decision you'll make in this lifetime, is the choice to invite God's Son into your heart. Please choose wisely . . . *and* immediately.

4
ACTION

But prove yourselves doers of the word,
and not merely hearers who delude themselves.
JAMES 1:22 NASB

When something needs to be done, the best time to do it is now, not later. But we're tempted to do otherwise. When the task at hand is difficult or unpleasant, we're tempted to procrastinate. But procrastination is the enemy of progress and a stumbling block on the path to success.

If we are to be responsible believers, we must realize that it is never enough simply to hear the instructions of God; we must also live by them. And it is never enough to wait idly by while others do God's work here on earth; we, too, must act. Doing God's work is a responsibility that each of us must bear, and when we do, our loving heavenly Father rewards our efforts with a bountiful harvest.

So, if you'd like to jumpstart your career or your life, ask God to give you the strength and the wisdom to do first things first, even if the first thing is hard. And while you're at it, use this time-tested formula for success: employ less talk and more action. Why? Because actions indeed speak louder than words—always have, always will. And a thousand good intentions pale in comparison to a single good deed.

*Never fail to do something because
you don't feel like it. Sometimes you just have
to do it now, and you'll feel like it later.*
MARIE T. FREEMAN

*We spend our lives dreaming of the future,
not realizing that a little of it slips away every day.*
BARBARA JOHNSON

*There may be no trumpet sound
or loud applause when we make a right decision,
just a calm sense of resolution and peace.*
GLORIA GAITHER

*If you are facing a difficult task don't put it off.
If you do it will just keep tormenting you.*
JOYCE MEYER

Do the unpleasant work first and enjoy the rest of the day.
MARIE T. FREEMAN

More from God's Word

For the kingdom of God is not a matter of talk but of power.
1 Corinthians 4:20 HCSB

*Whenever we have the opportunity, we should do good
to everyone—especially to our those in the family of faith.*
Galatians 6:10 NLT

*Therefore, with your minds ready for action,
be serious, and set your hope completely on the grace to be
brought to you at the revelation of Jesus Christ.*
1 Peter 1:13 HCSB

*When you make a vow to God, do not delay to fulfill it.
He has no pleasure in fools; fulfill your vow.*
Ecclesiastes 5:4 NIV

*Well done, good and faithful servant; you were faithful
over a few things, I will make you ruler over many things.
Enter into the joy of your lord.*
Matthew 25:21 NKJV

A Timely Tip

God's Word teaches us to be doers of the Word, not merely
hearers. And the best time to do God's work is now.

5

ADVERSITY

We are hard-pressed on every side, yet not crushed;
we are perplexed, but not in despair.
2 CORINTHIANS 4:8 NKJV

Tough times. Disappointments. Hardship. Pain. These experiences are the inevitable cost that each of us must pay for being human. From time to time, we all encounter adversity. Thankfully, we need never encounter it alone. God is always with us.

When we are troubled, God stands ready and willing to protect us. Our responsibility, of course, is to ask Him for protection. When we call upon Him in prayer, He will answer—in His own time and in His own way.

If you find yourself enduring difficult circumstances, remember that God remains in His heaven. If you become discouraged with the direction of your day or your life, turn your thoughts and prayers to Him. He is a God of possibility, not negativity. He will guide you through your difficulties and beyond them. And then, with a renewed spirit of optimism and hope, you can thank the Giver for gifts that are simply too numerous to count.

*Often the trials we mourn are really gateways
into the good things we long for.*
HANNAH WHITALL SMITH

*Allow God to use the difficulties and disappointments
in life as polish to transform your faith into a glistening
diamond that takes in and reflects His love.*
ELIZABETH GEORGE

*Recently I've been learning that life comes down to this:
God is in everything. Regardless of what difficulties I am
experiencing at the moment, or what things aren't as I
would like them to be, I look at the circumstances and say,
"Lord, what are You trying to teach me?"*
CATHERINE MARSHALL

If God sends us on stony paths, He provides strong shoes.
CORRIE TEN BOOM

*Often God shuts a door in our face so that He can
open the door through which He wants us to go.*
CATHERINE MARSHALL

More from God's Word

I called to the LORD in my distress; I called to my God.
From His temple He heard my voice.
2 SAMUEL 22:7 HCSB

God blesses the people who patiently endure testing
and temptation. Afterward they will receive the crown
of life that God has promised to those who love him.
JAMES 1:12 NLT

The LORD is my rock, my fortress, and my deliverer,
my God, my mountain where I seek refuge. My shield, the horn
of my salvation, my stronghold, my refuge, and my Savior.
2 SAMUEL 22:2–3 HCSB

He heals the brokenhearted and binds up their wounds.
PSALM 147:3 HCSB

The LORD is my shepherd; I shall not want.
PSALM 23:1 KJV

A Timely Tip

When tough times arrive and you're tempted to give in or give up, don't. Instead, work hard and pray harder. Better days may be just around the corner.

6

ANGER

Everyone must be quick to hear, slow to speak, and slow to anger, for man's anger does not accomplish God's righteousness.
JAMES 1:19–20 HCSB

The frustrations of everyday living can sometimes get the better of us, and we allow minor disappointments to cause us major problems. When we allow ourselves to become overly irritated by the inevitable ups and downs of life, we become overstressed, overheated, over-anxious, and just plain angry.

When you allow yourself to become angry, you are certain to defeat at least one person: yourself. When you allow the minor frustrations of everyday life to hijack your emotions, you do harm to yourself and to your loved ones. So today and every day, guard yourself against the kind of angry thinking that inevitably takes a toll on your emotions and your relationships.

As the old saying goes, "Anger usually improves nothing but the arch of a cat's back." So don't allow feelings of anger or frustration to rule your life, or, for that matter, your day. Your life is simply too short for that, and you deserve much better treatment than that . . . from yourself.

Anger unresolved will only bring you woe.
KAY ARTHUR

Life is too short to spend it being angry, bored, or dull.
BARBARA JOHNSON

*When something robs you of your peace of mind,
ask yourself if it is worth the energy you are expending on it.
If not, then put it out of your mind in an act of discipline.
Every time the thought of "it" returns, refuse it.*
KAY ARTHUR

*The hard part about being a praying wife is maintaining
a pure heart. If you have resentment, anger, unforgiveness,
or an ungodly attitude—even if there's good reason for it—
you'll have a difficult time seeing answers to your prayers.
But if you can release those feelings to God in total honesty,
there is nothing that can change a marriage more dramatically.*
STORMIE OMARTIAN

*If your temper gets the best of you . . .
then other people get to see the worst in you.*
MARIE T. FREEMAN

More from God's Word

*But I tell you that anyone who is angry
with a brother or sister will be subject to judgment.*
MATTHEW 5:22 NIV

*A hot-tempered man stirs up conflict,
but a man slow to anger calms strife.*
PROVERBS 15:18 HCSB

*He who is slow to wrath has great understanding,
but he who is impulsive exalts folly.*
PROVERBS 14:29 NKJV

*But now you must also put away all the following: anger,
wrath, malice, slander, and filthy language from your mouth.*
COLOSSIANS 3:8 HCSB

*Do not let the sun go down on your anger,
and do not give the devil an opportunity.*
EPHESIANS 4:26–27 NASB

A Timely Tip

Angry outbursts can be dangerous to your emotional and spiritual health, not to mention your relationships. So treat anger as an uninvited guest, and usher it away as quickly—and as quietly—as possible.

7

ARGUMENTS

Do everything without grumbling and arguing,
so that you may be blameless and pure.
PHILIPPIANS 2:14–15 HCSB

Time and again, God's Word warns us against angry outbursts and needless arguments. Arguments are seldom won but often lost, so when we acquire the unfortunate habit of habitual bickering, we do harm to our friends, to our families, to our coworkers, and to ourselves. And when we engage in petty squabbles, our losses usually outpace our gains.

Most arguments are a monumental waste of time and energy. And most squabbles do more for the devil than they do for God. So the next time you're tempted to engage in a silly squabble, slow down, catch your breath, and hold your tongue. When you do, you'll most certainly please your heavenly Father, and you'll send the devil packing.

Grudges are like hand grenades;
it is wise to release them before they destroy you.
BARBARA JOHNSON

Any complaints, any grumblings,
any disputes or murmurings, any anxieties,
any worries, any resentments or anything
that hints of a raging torrent of bitterness—
these are the things God calls me to die to daily.
JONI EARECKSON TADA

Forgiveness is the economy of the heart.
Forgiveness saves the expense of anger,
the cost of hatred, the waste of spirits.
HANNAH MORE

Never persist in trying to set people right.
HANNAH WHITALL SMITH

If I wanted to punish an enemy it should
be by fastening on him the trouble
of constantly hating somebody.
HANNAH MORE

More from God's Word

If any man among you seem to be religious, and bridleth not his tongue, but deceiveth his own heart, this man's religion is vain.
JAMES 1:26 KJV

A soft answer turneth away wrath:
but grievous words stir up anger.
PROVERBS 15:1 KJV

I tell you that on the day of judgment people
will have to account for every careless word they speak.
For by your words you will be acquitted,
and by your words you will be condemned.
MATTHEW 12:36–37 HCSB

People with quick tempers cause trouble,
but those who control their tempers stop a quarrel.
PROVERBS 15:18 NCV

Avoiding a fight is a mark of honor;
only fools insist on quarreling.
PROVERBS 20:3 NLT

A Timely Tip

If you "win" an argument, what have you really accomplished? Not much! So think twice (or thrice) before you allow yourself to be dragged into a disagreement that's not worth disagreeing about.

8

ASKING GOD

Ask, and it will be given to you; seek, and you will find;
knock, and it will be opened to you. For every one
who asks receives, and he who seeks finds,
and to him who knocks it shall be opened.

MATTHEW 7:7–8 NASB

God invites us to ask Him for the things we need, and He promises to hear our prayers as well as our thoughts. The Lord is always available and He's always ready to help us. And He knows precisely what we need. But He still instructs us to ask.

Do you make a habit of asking God for the things you need? Hopefully so. After all, the Father most certainly has a plan for your life. And, He can do great things through you if you have the courage to ask for His guidance and His help. So be fervent in prayer and don't hesitate to ask the Creator for the tools you need to accomplish His plan for your life. Then, get busy and expect the best. When you do your part, God will most certainly do His part. And great things are bound to happen.

God will help us become the people we are meant to be,
if only we will ask Him.
HANNAH WHITALL SMITH

When trials come your way—as inevitably they will—
do not run away. Run to your God and Father.
KAY ARTHUR

Often I have made a request of God with earnest pleadings
even backed up with Scripture, only to have Him say "No"
because He had something better in store.
RUTH BELL GRAHAM

By asking in Jesus' name, we're making a request not only
in His authority, but also for His interests and His benefit.
SHIRLEY DOBSON

When you ask God to do something,
don't ask timidly; put your whole heart into it.
MARIE T. FREEMAN

More from God's Word

Until now you have asked for nothing in My name.
Ask and you will receive, that your joy may be complete.
JOHN 16:24 HCSB

The effective prayer of a righteous man can accomplish much.
JAMES 5:16 NASB

Do not be anxious about anything, but in everything,
by prayer and petition, with thanksgiving,
present your requests to God.
PHILIPPIANS 4:6 NIV

Your Father knows the things you
have need of before you ask Him.
MATTHEW 6:8 NKJV

You did not choose me, but I chose you and appointed
you so that you might go and bear fruit—fruit that will last—
and so that whatever you ask in my name the Father will give you.
JOHN 15:16 NIV

A Timely Tip

If you want more from life, ask more from God. If you're pursuing a worthy goal, ask for God's help—and keep asking—until He answers your prayers.

9

ATTITUDE

*Finally, brothers, rejoice. Be restored, be encouraged,
be of the same mind, be at peace, and the God of love
and peace will be with you.*
2 CORINTHIANS 13:11 HCSB

Attitudes are the mental filters through which we view and interpret the world around us. People with positive attitudes look for the best and usually find it. People burdened by chronically negative attitudes are not so fortunate.

Your attitude will inevitably determine the quality and direction of your day and your life. That's why it's so important to stay positive.

The Christian life can be, and should be, cause for celebration. After all, every new day is a gift, every new circumstance an opportunity to praise and to serve. So how will you direct your thoughts today? Will you focus on God's love? Will you hold fast to His promises and trust His plan for your life? Or will you allow your thoughts to be hijacked by negativity and doubt. If you're a thoughtful believer, you'll think optimistically about yourself and your future. And while you're at it, you'll give thanks to the Creator for more blessings than you can count.

Preoccupy my thoughts with your praise beginning today.
JONI EARECKSON TADA

Attitude is the mind's paintbrush;
it can color any situation.
BARBARA JOHNSON

As we have by faith said no to sin,
so we should by faith say yes to God
and set our minds on things above,
where Christ is seated in the heavenlies.
VONETTE BRIGHT

No more imperfect thoughts.
No more sad memories.
No more ignorance. My redeemed body
will have a redeemed mind. Grant me a foretaste
of that perfect mind as You mirror Your thoughts in me today.
JONI EARECKSON TADA

The things we think are the things that feed our souls.
If we think on pure and lovely things, we shall grow pure
and lovely like them; and the converse is equally true.
HANNAH WHITALL SMITH

More from God's Word

A merry heart makes a cheerful countenance.
PROVERBS 15:13 NKJV

Be glad and rejoice,
because your reward is great in heaven.
MATTHEW 5:12 HCSB

You must have the same attitude that Christ Jesus had.
PHILIPPIANS 2:5 NLT

Rejoice always; pray without ceasing.
1 THESSALONIANS 5:16–17 NASB

This is the day the LORD has made;
let us rejoice and be glad in it.
PSALM 118:24 HCSB

A Timely Tip

As a Christian, you have every reason on earth—and in heaven—to have a positive attitude. After all, God's in charge, He loves you, and He's prepared a place for you to live eternally with Him. And that's what really matters.

10

BIBLE STUDY

*All Scripture is given by inspiration of God,
and is profitable for doctrine, for reproof, for correction,
for instruction in righteousness.*

2 TIMOTHY 3:16 KJV

The promises found in God's Word are the cornerstone of the Christian faith. We must trust those promises and build our lives upon them.

The Bible is a priceless gift—a tool for Christians to use every day, in every situation. Yet too many Christians put away their spiritual tool kits and rely instead on the world's promises. Unfortunately, the world makes promises it doesn't keep. God has no such record of failure. He keeps every single one of His promises. On Him you can depend.

So how will you respond to God's promises? Will you treat your Bible as a one-of-a-kind guidebook for life here on earth and life eternal in heaven? And, will you let your Creator speak to you through His Holy Word? Hopefully so because the Lord has given you all the tools you need to accomplish His plan for your life. He placed every instruction you'll need in the book He wrote. The rest is up to you.

Jesus is Victor. Calvary is the place of victory.
Obedience is the pathway of victory.
Bible study and prayer is the preparation for victory.
CORRIE TEN BOOM

The Bible is an ocean of instruction and wisdom.
Dip daily into the vast pool to discover its truths.
ELIZABETH GEORGE

Gather the riches of God's promises.
Nobody can take away from you those texts
from the Bible which you have learned by heart.
CORRIE TEN BOOM

Dust off that Bible.
It has the answers you are looking for,
and its delights await you.
ELIZABETH GEORGE

If we neglect the Bible, we cannot expect
to benefit from the wisdom and direction
that result from knowing God's Word.
VONETTE BRIGHT

More from God's Word

*The counsel of the LORD stands forever, the plans
of His heart from generation to generation.*
PSALM 33:11 NASB

*But whoever looks intently into the perfect law that gives
freedom, and continues in it—not forgetting what they have
heard, but doing it—they will be blessed in what they do.*
JAMES 1:25 NIV

*But the word of the Lord endures forever. And this is the word
that was preached as the gospel to you.*
1 PETER 1:25 HCSB

*But grow in the grace and knowledge of our Lord
and Savior Jesus Christ. To Him be the glory
both now and to the day of eternity.*
2 PETER 3:18 HCSB

*You will be a good servant of Christ Jesus,
nourished by the words of the faith and of the good
teaching that you have followed.*
1 TIMOTHY 4:6 HCSB

A Timely Tip

Even if you've studied the Bible for many years, you've still got
lots to learn. Bible study should be a lifelong endeavor. Make it *your*
lifelong endeavor.

11

BITTERNESS

Let all bitterness, wrath, anger, clamor,
and evil speaking be put away from you, with all malice.
And be kind to one another, tenderhearted, forgiving
one another, just as God in Christ forgave you.
EPHESIANS 4:31–32 NKJV

Bitterness is a spiritual sickness. It will consume your soul; it is dangerous to your emotional health; it can destroy you if you let it. So don't let it!

The world holds few if any rewards for those who remain angrily focused upon the past. Still, the act of forgiveness is difficult for all but the most saintly men and women. Being frail, fallible, imperfect human beings, most of us are quick to anger, quick to blame, slow to forgive, and even slower to forget. Yet we know that it's best to forgive others, just as we, too, have been forgiven.

If there exists even one person—including yourself—against whom you still harbor bitter feelings, it's time to forgive and move on. Bitterness and regret are not part of God's plan for you, but God won't force you to forgive others. It's a job that only you can finish, and the sooner you finish it, the better.

If you are caught up in intense feelings of anger or resentment, you know all too well the destructive power of these emotions. How can you rid yourself of these feelings? First, you must prayerfully ask God to cleanse your heart. Then, you must learn to catch yourself whenever thoughts of bitterness or hatred begin to attack you. Your challenge is this: Learn to resist negative thoughts before they hijack your emotions. When you learn to direct your thoughts toward more positive topics, you'll be protected from the spiritual and emotional consequences of bitterness. And you'll be a wiser, healthier, happier woman, too.

Grudges are like hand grenades;
It is wise to release them before they destroy you.
BARBARA JOHNSON

Bitterness is a spiritual cancer, a rapidly
growing malignancy that can consume your life.
Bitterness cannot be ignored but must be healed
at the very core, and only Christ can heal bitterness.
BETH MOORE

Sin is any deed or memory that hampers
or binds human personality.
CATHERINE MARSHALL

Forgiveness is the key that unlocks the door of resentment
and the handcuffs of hate. It is a power that breaks
the chains of bitterness and the shackles of selfishness.
CORRIE TEN BOOM

Bitterness is the price we charge ourselves
for being unwilling to forgive.
MARIE T. FREEMAN

More from God's Word

*Do all things without complaining and disputing,
that you may become blameless and harmless, children of God
without fault in the midst of a crooked and perverse generation,
among whom you shine as lights in the world.*
PHILIPPIANS 2:14–15 NKJV

*But when you are praying, first forgive anyone
you are holding a grudge against, so that your
Father in heaven will forgive your sins, too.*
MARK 11:25 NLT

*Do not repay anyone evil for evil.
Try to do what is honorable in everyone's eyes.*
ROMANS 12:17 HCSB

*The heart knows its own bitterness,
and a stranger does not share its joy.*
PROVERBS 14:10 NKJV

*Do not judge, and you will not be judged.
Do not condemn, and you will not be condemned.
Forgive, and you will be forgiven.*
LUKE 6:37 HCSB

A Timely Tip

The Bible warns that bitterness is both dangerous and self-destructive. So today, make a list of the people you need to forgive and the things you need to forget. Then, ask God to give you the strength to forgive and move on.

12

BLESSINGS

The LORD bless you and keep you; the LORD make His face shine upon you, and be gracious to you.
NUMBERS 6:24–25 HCSB

Because we have been so richly blessed, we should make thanksgiving a habit, a regular part of our daily routines. But sometimes, amid the demands and obligations of everyday life, we may allow the interruptions and distractions of everyday life to interfere with the time we spend with God.

Have you counted your blessings today? And have you thanked God for them? Hopefully so. After all, God's gifts include your family, your friends, your talents, your opportunities, your possessions, and the priceless gift of eternal life. How glorious are these gifts, and God is responsible for every one of them.

So today, as you go about the duties of everyday life, pause and give thanks to the Creator. He deserves your praise, and you deserve the experience of praising Him.

We do not need to beg Him to bless us;
He simply cannot help it.
HANNAH WHITALL SMITH

Every difficult task that comes across your path—
every one that you would rather not do, that will take
the most effort, cause the most pain, and be the greatest struggle—
brings a blessing with it.
LETTIE COWMAN

How ridiculous to grasp for future gifts when today's
is set before you. Receive today's gift gratefully,
unwrapping it tenderly and delving into its depths.
SARAH YOUNG

Do we not continually pass by blessings innumerable
without notice, and instead fix our eyes on our trials
and our losses? And, do we not talk about our trials until
we almost begin to think we have no blessings at all?
HANNAH WHITALL SMITH

God's gifts put men's best dreams to shame.
ELIZABETH BARRETT BROWNING

More from God's Word

You will show me the path of life; in Your presence is fullness of joy; at Your right hand are pleasures forevermore.
PSALM 16:11 NKJV

The Lord is my rock, my fortress, and my deliverer, my God, my mountain where I seek refuge. My shield, the horn of my salvation, my stronghold, my refuge, and my Savior.
2 SAMUEL 22:2–3 HCSB

The LORD is good to all: and his tender mercies are over all his works.
PSALM 145:9 KJV

The LORD is my shepherd; I shall not want.
PSALM 23:1 KJV

Blessings crown the head of the righteous.
PROVERBS 10:6 NIV

A Timely Tip

God has given you more blessings than you can possibly count, but it doesn't hurt to begin counting them. And while you're at it, don't forget to praise the Giver of these incalculable gifts.

13

CELEBRATION

Rejoice in the Lord always. Again I will say, rejoice!
PHILIPPIANS 4:4 NKJV

Each day contains cause for celebration. And each day has its own share of blessings. Our assignment, as grateful believers, is to look for the blessings and celebrate them.

Today, like every other day, is a priceless gift from God. He has offered us yet another opportunity to serve Him with smiling faces and willing hands. When we do our part, He inevitably does His part, and miracles happen.

The Lord has promised to bless you and keep you, now and forever. So, don't wait for birthdays or holidays. Make this day an exciting adventure. And while you're at it, take time to thank God for His blessings. He deserves your gratitude, and you deserve the joy of expressing it.

Christ is the secret, the source, the substance, the center,
and the circumference of all true and lasting gladness.
LETTIE COWMAN

When the dream of our heart is one that God has planted there,
a strange happiness flows into us. At that moment, all of the
spiritual resources of the universe are released to help us.
Our praying is then at one with the will of God and becomes
a channel for the Creator's purposes for us and our world.
CATHERINE MARSHALL

Joy is a by-product not of happy circumstances, education,
or talent, but of a healthy relationship with God
and a determination to love Him no matter what.
BARBARA JOHNSON

God knows everything. He can manage everything,
and He loves us. Surely this is enough for a fullness
of joy that is beyond words.
HANNAH WHITALL SMITH

According to Jesus, it is God's will that
His children be filled with the joy of life.
CATHERINE MARSHALL

More from God's Word

A happy heart is like a continual feast.
PROVERBS 15:15 NCV

Rejoice always, pray without ceasing,
in everything give thanks; for this is the will
of God in Christ Jesus for you.
1 THESSALONIANS 5:16–18 NKJV

This is the day which the LORD has made;
let us rejoice and be glad in it.
PSALM 118:24 NASB

I delight greatly in the LORD;
my soul rejoices in my God.
ISAIAH 61:10 NIV

I came that they may have life,
and have it abundantly.
JOHN 10:10 NASB

A Timely Tip

Every day is a glorious opportunity to celebrate life by loving your neighbor and serving your Creator. Join the celebration.

14
CHEERFULNESS

A cheerful heart has a continual feast.
PROVERBS 15:15 HCSB

As Christians, we have so many reasons to be cheerful: God is in His heaven; He remains firmly in control; He loves us; and through His Son, He has offered us a path to eternal life. Despite these blessings, all of us will occasionally fall victim to the inevitable frustrations of everyday life. When we do, we should pause, take a deep breath, and remember how richly we've been blessed.

Cheerfulness is a gift that we give to others and to ourselves. The joy we give to others is reciprocal: whatever we give away is returned to us, oftentimes in greater measure. So make this promise to yourself and keep it: be a cheerful ambassador for Christ. He deserves no less, and neither, for that matter, do you.

*Focus on giving smiles away and you will always discover
that your own smiles will always be in great supply!*

JOYCE MEYER

*When we bring sunshine into the lives of others,
we're warmed by it ourselves.
When we spill a little happiness, it splashes on us.*

BARBARA JOHNSON

*God is good, and heaven is forever.
And if those two facts don't cheer you up, nothing will.*

MARIE T. FREEMAN

*When the dream of our heart is one that
God has planted there, a strange happiness flows into us.
At that moment, the spiritual resources
of the universe are released to help us.*

CATHERINE MARSHALL

*If we are going to experience joy in this lifetime,
there's only one possible way: We have to choose it.
We will to choose it in the middle of a situation
that seems too hard to bear. We have to choose it
even if our worst nightmare comes true.*

KAY WARREN

More from God's Word

Rejoice always, pray without ceasing, in everything give thanks;
for this is the will of God in Christ Jesus for you.
1 Thessalonians 5:16-18 NKJV

Shout for joy to the Lord, all the earth. Worship the Lord with
gladness; come before him with joyful songs.
Psalm 100:1–2 NIV

This is the day that the Lord has made.
Let us rejoice and be glad today!
Psalm 118:24 NCV

Do everything without grumbling and arguing,
so that you may be blameless and pure.
Philippians 2:14–15 HCSB

A cheerful heart is good medicine,
but a crushed spirit dries up the bones.
Proverbs 17:22 NIV

A Timely Tip

Cheerfulness is its own reward, but not its only reward. When you sow a positive attitude, you'll reap a positive life.

15
CHRIST'S LOVE

As the Father loved Me, I also have loved you;
abide in My love.
JOHN 15:9 NKJV

How much does Christ love us? More than we, as mere mortals, can comprehend. His love is perfect and steadfast. Even though we are fallible and wayward, the Good Shepherd cares for us still. Even though we have fallen far short of the Father's commandments, Christ loves us with a power and depth that are beyond our understanding. The sacrifice that Jesus made upon the cross was made for each of us, and His love endures to the edge of eternity and beyond.

Christ's love changes everything. When you accept His gift of grace, you are transformed, not only for today, but also for all eternity. If you haven't already done so, accept Jesus Christ as your Savior. He's waiting patiently for you to invite Him into your heart. Please don't make Him wait a single minute longer.

To God be the glory, great things He has done;
So loved He the world that He gave us His Son.

FANNY CROSBY

Live your lives in love, the same sort of love
which Christ gives us, and which He perfectly expressed
when He gave Himself as a sacrifice to God.

CORRIE TEN BOOM

This hard place in which you perhaps find yourself
is the very place in which God is giving you opportunity
to look only to Him, to spend time in prayer,
and to learn long-suffering, gentleness, meekness—
in short, to learn the depths of the love
that Christ Himself has poured out on all of us.

ELISABETH ELLIOT

Sometimes Agape really hurts. It broke the heart of God
to demonstrate His love to us through
Christ but its ultimate end was salvation.

BETH MOORE

It has been the faith of the Son of God who loves me
and gave Himself for me that has held me in the darkest valley
and the hottest fires and the deepest waters.

ELISABETH ELLIOT

More from God's Word

*I am the good shepherd. The good shepherd
lays down his life for the sheep.*
JOHN 10:11 HCSB

*For Christ also suffered once for sins, the just for the unjust,
that He might bring us to God, being put to death
in the flesh but made alive by the Spirit.*
1 PETER 3:18 NKJV

*No one has greater love than this, that someone
would lay down his life for his friends.*
JOHN 15:13 HCSB

We love him, because he first loved us.
1 JOHN 4:19 KJV

*For God so loved the world, that he gave his
only begotten Son, that whosoever believeth in him
should not perish, but have everlasting life.*
JOHN 3:16 KJV

A Timely Tip

Christ's love is meant to be experienced—and shared—by you.

16
CIRCUMSTANCES

Trust in him at all times, you people;
pour out your hearts to him, for God is our refuge.
PSALM 62:8 NIV

All of us must endure difficult circumstances, those tough times when our faith is tested and our strength is stretched to the limit. We find ourselves in situations that we didn't ask for and probably don't deserve. During these difficult days, we try our best to "hold up under the circumstances." But God has a better plan. He intends for us to rise above our circumstances, and He's promised to help us do it.

Are you dealing with a difficult situation or a tough problem? Do you struggle with occasional periods of discouragement and doubt? Are you worried, weary, or downcast? If so, don't face tough times alone. Face them with God as your partner, your protector, and your guide. Talk to Him often, ask for His guidance, and listen carefully for His response. When you do, He will give you the strength to meet any challenge, the courage to face any problem, and the patience to endure—and to eventually rise above—any circumstance.

*Accept each day as it comes to you. Do not waste your time
and energy wishing for a different set of circumstances.*
SARAH YOUNG

*Jesus did not promise to change the circumstances around us.
He promised great peace and pure joy to those who would learn
to believe that God actually controls all things.*
CORRIE TEN BOOM

*The secret is Christ in me,
not me in a different set of circumstances.*
ELISABETH ELLIOT

*The only way to keep your balance is to fix your eyes
on the One who never changes. If you gaze too long at your
circumstances, you will become dizzy and confused.*
SARAH YOUNG

Subdue your heart to match your circumstances.
JONI EARECKSON TADA

More from God's Word

The Lord is a refuge for His people and a stronghold.
JOEL 3:16 NASB

Cast your burden on the Lord, and He shall sustain you;
He shall never permit the righteous to be moved.
PSALM 55:22 NKJV

The Lord is a refuge for the oppressed,
a refuge in times of trouble.
PSALM 9:9 HCSB

God is our protection and our strength.
He always helps in times of trouble.
PSALM 46:1 NCV

I have learned in whatever state I am, to be content.
PHILIPPIANS 4:11 NKJV

A Timely Tip

A change of circumstances is rarely as important as a change in attitude. If you change your thoughts, you will most certainly change your circumstances.

17
COMPLAINING

Be hospitable to one another without complaining.
1 PETER 4:9 HCSB

Most of us have more blessings than we can count, yet we still find things to complain about. To complain, of course, is not only shortsighted, but it is also a serious roadblock on the path to spiritual abundance. But in our weakest moments we still grumble, whine, and moan. Sometimes we give voice to our complaints, and on other occasions, we manage to keep our protestations to ourselves. But even when no one else hears our complaints, God does.

Would you like to feel more comfortable about your circumstances and your life? Then promise yourself that you'll do whatever it takes to ensure that you focus your thoughts and energy on the major blessings you've received, not the minor hardships you must occasionally endure.

So the next time you're tempted to complain about the inevitable frustrations of everyday living, don't do it. Today and every day, make it a practice to count your blessings, not your inconveniences. It's the truly decent way to live.

It is always possible to be thankful for what is given
rather than to complain about what is not given.
One or the other becomes a habit of life.
ELISABETH ELLIOT

Trust and thankfulness will get you safely through this day.
Trust protects you from worrying and obsessing. Thankfulness
keeps you from criticizing and complaining.
SARAH YOUNG

Thanksgiving or complaining—these words express two
contrasting attitudes of the souls of God's children.
The soul that gives thanks can find comfort in everything;
the soul that complains can find comfort in nothing.
HANNAH WHITALL SMITH

Any complaints, any grumblings, any disputes or murmurings,
any anxieties, any worries, any resentments or anything
that hints of a raging torrent of bitterness—
these are the things God calls me to die to daily.
JONI EARECKSON TADA

And, at the bottom, all complainings mean just this: that we do
not believe in God, and that we do not trust in His salvation.
HANNAH WHITALL SMITH

More from God's Word

Do everything without complaining or arguing.
Then you will be innocent and without any wrong.
PHILIPPIANS 2:14–15 NCV

A fool's displeasure is known at once,
but whoever ignores an insult is sensible.
PROVERBS 12:16 HCSB

Those who guard their lips preserve their lives,
but those who speak rashly will come to ruin.
PROVERBS 13:3 NIV

Those who consider themselves religious
and yet do not keep a tight rein on their tongues
deceive themselves, and their religion is worthless.
JAMES 1:26 NIV

My dear brothers and sisters,
always be willing to listen and slow to speak.
JAMES 1:19 NCV

A Timely Tip

If you feel a personal pity party coming on, slow down and start counting your blessings. If you fill your heart with gratitude, there's simply no room left for complaints.

18
CONFIDENCE

So we may boldly say: "The LORD is my helper;
I will not fear. What can man do to me?"
HEBREWS 13:6 NKJV

As Christians, we have every reason live confidently. After all, we've read God's promises and we know that He's prepared a place for us in heaven. And with God on our side, what should we fear? The answer, of course, is nothing. But sometimes, despite our faith and despite God's promises, we find ourselves gripped by earthly apprehensions.

When we focus on our doubts and fears, we can concoct a lengthy list of reasons to lie awake at night and fret about the uncertainties of the coming day. A better strategy, of course, is to focus, not upon our fears, but upon our God.

Are you a confident Christian? You should be. God's promises never fail and His love is everlasting. So the next time you need a boost of confidence, slow down and have a little chat with your Creator. Count your blessings, not your troubles. Focus on possibilities, not problems. And remember that with God on your side, you have absolutely nothing to fear.

Joy is the settled assurance that God is in control of all the details of my life, the quiet confidence that ultimately everything is going to be all right, and the determined choice to praise God in all things.

KAY WARREN

We don't need self-confidence; we need God-confidence.

JOYCE MEYER

God's all-sufficiency is a major. Your inability is a minor. Major in majors, not in minors.

CORRIE TEN BOOM

We need to recognize that lack of confidence does not equal humility. In fact, genuinely humble people have enormous confidence because it rests in a great God.

BETH MOORE

Never yield to gloomy anticipation. Place your hope and confidence in God. He has no record of failure.

LETTIE COWMAN

More from God's Word

You are my hope; O Lord GOD, You are my confidence.
PSALM 71:5 NASB

God is our refuge and strength,
a very present help in trouble.
PSALM 46:1 NKJV

I lift up my eyes to the hills—
where does my help come from?
My help comes from the LORD,
the Maker of heaven and earth.
PSALM 121:1–2 NIV

Be strong and courageous, and do the work.
Don't be afraid or discouraged, for the LORD God,
my God, is with you. He won't leave you or forsake you.
1 CHRONICLES 28:20 HCSB

In this world you will have trouble.
But take heart! I have overcome the world.
JOHN 16:33 NIV

A Timely Tip

As a Christian, you have every reason to be confident about your life, your future, and your eternal destiny. With God as your partner, you have nothing to fear.

19

CONSCIENCE

Now the goal of our instruction is love that comes from a pure heart, a good conscience, and a sincere faith.
1 TIMOTHY 1:5 HCSB

God has given each of us a conscience, and He intends for us to use it. But sometimes we don't. Instead of listening to that quiet inner voice that warns us against disobedience and danger, we're tempted to rush headlong into situations that we soon come to regret.

God promises that He rewards good conduct and that He blesses those who obey His Word. The Lord also issues a stern warning to those who rebel against His commandments. Wise women heed that warning. Count yourself among their number.

Sometime soon, perhaps today, your conscience will speak; when it does, listen carefully. God may be trying to get a message through to you. Don't miss it.

*God desires that we become spiritually healthy enough
through faith to have a conscience that rightly
interprets the work of the Holy Spirit.*
BETH MOORE

*It is in stillness that the Voice will be heard,
the only voice in all the universe that speaks
peace to the deepest part of us.*
ELISABETH ELLIOT

*Whatever weakens your reason, impairs the tenderness
of your conscience, obscures your sense of God, or takes
off your relish of spiritual things, that thing is sin to you.*
SUSANNA WESLEY

*I believe that in every time and place it is within
our power to acquiesce in the will of God—
and what peace it brings to do so!*
ELISABETH ELLIOT

*Mark it down—your progress in holiness will never exceed
your relationship with the holy Word of God.*
NANCY LEIGH DEMOSS

More from God's Word

So I strive always to keep my conscience
clear before God and man.
ACTS 24:16 NIV

People's thoughts can be like a deep well,
but someone with understanding can find the wisdom there.
PROVERBS 20:5 NCV

Let us come near to God with a sincere heart and a sure faith,
because we have been made free from a guilty conscience,
and our bodies have been washed with pure water.
HEBREWS 10:22 NCV

Create in me a clean heart, O God;
and renew a right spirit within me.
PSALM 51:10 KJV

Behold, the kingdom of God is within you.
LUKE 17:21 KJV

A Timely Tip

The bigger the decision, the more carefully you should listen to your conscience. The bigger the choice, the more carefully you should listen to His voice.

20
CONTENTMENT

I have learned in whatever state I am, to be content.
PHILIPPIANS 4:11 NKJV

Everywhere we turn, or so it seems, the world promises us contentment and happiness. We are bombarded by messages offering us the "good life" if only we will purchase products and services that are designed to provide happiness, success, and contentment. But the contentment that the world offers is fleeting and incomplete. Thankfully, the contentment that God offers is all-encompassing and everlasting.

Happiness depends less upon our circumstances than upon our thoughts. When we turn our thoughts to God, to His gifts, and to His glorious creation, we experience the joy that God intends for His children. But, when we focus on the negative aspects of life—or when we disobey God's commandments—we cause ourselves needless suffering.

Do you sincerely want to be a contented Christian? Then set your mind and your heart upon God's love and His grace. Seek first the salvation that is available through a personal relationship with Jesus Christ, and then claim the joy, the contentment, and the spiritual abundance that God offers His children.

*We will never be happy until we make God the source
of our fulfillment and the answer to our longings.*
STORMIE OMARTIAN

*If I could just hang in there, being faithful to my own tasks,
God would make me joyful and content.
The responsibility is mine, but the power is His.*
PEG RANKIN

*The key to contentment is to consider.
Consider who you are and be satisfied with that.
Consider what you have and be satisfied with that.
Consider what God's doing and be satisfied with that.*
LUCI SWINDOLL

*When we are set free from the bondage of pleasing others,
when we are free from currying others' favor and others'
approval—then no one will be able to make us miserable
or dissatisfied. And then, if we know we have pleased God,
contentment will be our consolation.*
KAY ARTHUR

*Those who are God's without reserve are,
in every sense, content.*
HANNAH WHITALL SMITH

MORE FROM GOD'S WORD

But godliness with contentment is a great gain.
1 TIMOTHY 6:6 HCSB

A tranquil heart is life to the body,
but jealousy is rottenness to the bones.
PROVERBS 14:30 HCSB

Make sure that your character is free from the love of money,
being content with what you have; for He Himself has said,
"I will never desert you, nor will I ever forsake you."
HEBREWS 13:5 NASB

Come unto me, all ye that labor and are heavy laden,
and I will give you rest.
MATTHEW 11:28 KJV

The peace of God, which passeth all understanding,
shall keep your hearts and minds through Christ Jesus.
PHILIPPIANS 4:7 KJV

A TIMELY TIP

Contentment comes, not from your circumstances, but from your attitude and your faith. So stay positive and remember that faith is the foundation of a contented life.

21

COURAGE

*Be strong and courageous, and do the work. Do not be afraid
or discouraged, for the LORD God, my God, is with you.*
1 CHRONICLES 28:20 NIV

As believers in a risen Christ, we can, and should, live courageously. After all, Jesus promises us that He has overcome the world and that He has made a place for us in heaven. So we have nothing to fear in the long term because our Lord will care for us throughout eternity. But what about those short-term, everyday worries that keep us up at night? And what about the life-altering hardships that leave us wondering if we can ever recover? The answer, of course, is that because God cares for us in good times and hard times, we can turn our concerns over to Him in prayer, knowing that all things ultimately work for the good of those who love Him.

When you form a one-on-one relationship with your Creator, you can be comforted by the fact that wherever you find yourself, whether at the top of the mountain or the depths of the valley, God is there with you. And because your Creator cares for you and protects you, you can rise above your fears.

At this very moment the Lord is seeking to work in you and through you. He's asking you to live abundantly and courageously, and He's ready to help. Now.

*Just as courage is faith in good, so discouragement
is faith in evil, and, while courage opens the door to good,
discouragement opens it to evil.*
HANNAH WHITALL SMITH

*We look at our burdens and heavy loads,
and we shrink from them. But, if we lift them
and bind them about our hearts, they become wings,
and on them we can rise and soar toward God.*
LETTIE COWMAN

Just pray for a tough hide and a tender heart.
RUTH BELL GRAHAM

*Do not limit the limitless God! With Him,
face the future unafraid because you are never alone.*
LETTIE COWMAN

*Every difficult task that comes across your path—
every one that you would rather not do,
that will take the most effort, cause the most pain,
and be the greatest struggle—brings a blessing with it.*
LETTIE COWMAN

More from God's Word

Be on guard. Stand firm in the faith.
Be courageous. Be strong.
1 Corinthians 16:13 NLT

I can do all things through Him who strengthens me.
Philippians 4:13 NASB

For God has not given us a spirit of fearfulness,
but one of power, love, and sound judgment.
2 Timothy 1:7 HCSB

But He said to them, "It is I; do not be afraid."
John 6:20 NKJV

Behold, God is my salvation;
I will trust, and not be afraid.
Isaiah 12:2 KJV

A Timely Tip

Is your courage being tested today? If so, hold fast to God's promises and pray. God will give you the strength to meet any challenge if you ask Him sincerely and often. So ask.

22

COURTESY

Let everyone see that you are gentle and kind.
The Lord is coming soon.
PHILIPPIANS 4:5 NCV

Did Christ instruct us in matters of etiquette and courtesy? Of course He did. Christ's instructions are clear: "In everything, therefore, treat people the same way you want them to treat you, for this is the Law and the Prophets" (Matthew 7:12 NASB). Jesus did not say, "In some things, treat people as you wish to be treated." And He did not say, "From time to time, treat others with kindness." Christ said that we should treat others as we wish to be treated in every aspect of our daily lives. This, of course, is a tall order indeed, but as Christians, we are commanded to do our best.

Today, be a little kinder than necessary to family members, friends, and total strangers. And, as you consider all the things that Christ has done in your life, honor Him with your words and with your deeds. He expects no less, and He deserves no less.

The Golden Rule starts at home,
but it should never stop there.
MARIE T. FREEMAN

The goodness you receive from God
is a treasure for you to share with others.
ELIZABETH GEORGE

Kindness in this world will do much to help others,
not only to come into the light,
but also to grow in grace day by day.
FANNY CROSBY

The best times in life are made
a thousand times better
when shared with a dear friend.
LUCI SWINDOLL

Courtesy is contagious.
MARIE T. FREEMAN

More from God's Word

So, my friends, when you come together to the Lord's Table,
be reverent and courteous with one another.
1 CORINTHIANS 11:33 MSG

Kind words are like honey—
sweet to the soul and healthy for the body.
PROVERBS 16:24 NLT

Kind people do themselves a favor,
but cruel people bring trouble on themselves.
PROVERBS 11:17 NCV

Do not neglect to show hospitality to strangers,
for by this some have entertained angels without knowing it.
HEBREWS 13:2 NASB

Finally, all of you be of one mind, having compassion for one
another; love as brothers, be tenderhearted, be courteous.
1 PETER 3:8 NKJV

A Timely Tip

If you're a Christian, courtesy isn't optional. If you disagree, do so without being disagreeable; if you're angry, hold your tongue; if you're frustrated or tired, don't argue. Instead, put yourself in time-out until the anger subsides.

23

DECISIONS

But if any of you needs wisdom, you should ask God for it.
He is generous to everyone and will
give you wisdom without criticizing you.

JAMES 1:5 NCV

Decisions, decisions, decisions. So many decisions to make, and with so little information. Yet decide we must. The stories of our lives are, quite literally, human dramas woven together by the habits we form and the choices we make.

The quality of the decisions you make today will determine, to a surprising extent, the quality of this particular day *and* the direction of all the ones that follow it.

Are you willing to invest the time, the effort, and the prayers that are required to make wise decisions? Are you willing to take your concerns to God and to avail yourself of the messages and mentors He has placed along your path? If you answered yes to these questions, you'll most certainly make better decisions, decisions that, by the way, will lead directly and inexorably to a better life.

*Your choices and decisions are a reflection of how well
you've set and followed your priorities.*
ELIZABETH GEORGE

*The Reference Point for the Christian is the Bible.
All values, judgments, and attitudes must be gauged
in relationship to this Reference Point.*
RUTH BELL GRAHAM

Make no decision without prayer!
ELIZABETH GEORGE

*There may be no trumpet sound or loud applause
when we make a right decision,
just a calm sense of resolution and peace.*
GLORIA GAITHER

*God is voting for us all the time.
The devil is voting against us all the time.
The way we vote carries the election.*
CORRIE TEN BOOM

More from God's Word

In every way be an example of doing good deeds.
When you teach, do it with honesty and seriousness.
TITUS 2:7 NCV

Blessed is the man who walks not in the counsel
of the ungodly, nor stands in the path of sinners,
nor sits in the seat of the scornful.
PSALM 1:1 NKJV

We can make our own plans, but the LORD
gives the right answer. People may be pure in their own eyes,
but the LORD examines their motives.
PROVERBS 16:1–2 NLT

The highway of the upright avoids evil;
the one who guards his way protects his life.
PROVERBS 16:17 HCSB

By their fruits ye shall know them.
MATTHEW 7:20 KJV

A Timely Tip

Today and every day, remember that every step of your life's journey is a choice, and the overall quality of your decisions will help determine the overall quality of the journey.

24

DEVOTIONAL

Morning by morning he wakens me and opens my understanding to his will. The Sovereign LORD has spoken to me, and I have listened.

ISAIAH 50:4–5 NLT

Every new day is a gift from the Creator, a gift that allows each of us to say "thank You" by spending time with the Giver. When we begin the day with our Bibles open and our hearts attuned to God, we are inevitably blessed by the promises we find in His Word.

During the quiet moments we spend with the Lord, He guides us; He leads us; and He touches our hearts. These are precious moments that contribute to our spiritual growth. We need our daily devotions.

Each day of your life has 1,440 minutes, and God deserves a few of them. And, you deserve the experience of spending a few quiet minutes every morning with your Creator. So, if you haven't already done so, establish the habit of spending time with God every day of the week. It's a habit that will change your day and revolutionize your life. When you give the Lord your undivided attention, everything changes, including you.

Begin each day with God. It will change your priorities.
ELIZABETH GEORGE

*I believe the reason so many are failing today
is that they have not disciplined themselves to read
God's Word consistently, day in and day out,
and to apply it to every situation in life.*
KAY ARTHUR

*Don't pray when you feel like it.
Have an appointment with the Lord and keep it.*
CORRIE TEN BOOM

*I think that God required the Israelites to gather manna every
morning so that they would learn to come to Him daily.*
CYNTHIA HEALD

*Faithful prayer warriors and devoted Bible lovers
will tell you that their passion for disciplined
quiet time with the Lord is not a sign of strength
but an admission of weakness—a hard-earned
realization that they are nothing on their own
compared with who they are after they've been with Him.*
DORIS GREIG

MORE FROM GOD'S WORD

It is good to give thanks to the LORD,
and to sing praises to Your name, O Most High.
PSALM 92:1 NKJV

Thy word is a lamp unto my feet, and a light unto my path.
PSALM 119:105 KJV

Heaven and earth will pass away,
but My words will never pass away.
MATTHEW 24:35 HCSB

Early the next morning, while it was still dark,
Jesus woke and left the house.
He went to a lonely place, where he prayed.
MARK 1:35 NCV

But grow in the grace and knowledge
of our Lord and Savior Jesus Christ. To Him be the glory
both now and to the day of eternity.
2 PETER 3:18 HCSB

A TIMELY TIP

You need a regular appointment with your Creator. God is ready to talk to you, and you should prepare yourself each morning to talk to Him.

25

DISAPPOINTMENTS

He heals the brokenhearted and binds up their wounds.
PSALM 147:3 HCSB

As we make the journey from the cradle to the grave, disappointments are inevitable. No matter how competent we are, no matter how fortunate, we still encounter circumstances that fall far short of our expectations. When tough times arrive, we have choices to make: we can feel sorry for ourselves, or we can get angry, or we can become depressed. Or, we can get busy praying about out problems and solving them.

When we are disheartened—on those cloudy days when our strength is sapped and our hope is shaken—there exists a source from which we can draw perspective and courage. That source is God. When we turn everything over to Him, we find that He is sufficient to meet our needs. No problem is too big for Him.

So, the next time you feel discouraged, slow down long enough to have a serious talk with your Creator. Pray for guidance, pray for strength, and pray for the wisdom to trust your heavenly Father. Your troubles are temporary; His love is not.

*Allow God to use the difficulties and disappointments
in life as polish to transform your faith into a glistening
diamond that takes in and reflects His love.*

ELIZABETH GEORGE

*We all have sorrows and disappointments, but one must never
forget that, if commended to God, they will issue in good.
His own solution is far better than any we could conceive.*

FANNY CROSBY

*We must meet our disappointments, our malicious enemies,
our provoking friends, our trials of every sort,
with an attitude of surrender and trust. We must rise above
them in Christ so they lose their power to harm us.*

HANNAH WHITALL SMITH

*What do you do when disappointment comes?
When it weighs on you like a rock, you can either let it press
you down until you become discouraged, even devastated,
or you can use it as a stepping-stone to better things.*

JOYCE MEYER

*Why should I ever resist any delay or disappointment,
any affliction or oppression or humiliation when
I know God will use it in my life to make me
like Jesus and to prepare me for heaven?*

KAY ARTHUR

MORE FROM GOD'S WORD

Many adversities come to the one who is righteous,
but the LORD delivers him from them all.
PSALM 34:19 HCSB

He shall not be afraid of evil tidings:
his heart is fixed, trusting in the LORD.
PSALM 112:7 KJV

Do not despise the chastening of the Lord,
nor be discouraged when you are rebuked by Him.
HEBREWS 12:5 NKJV

They that sow in tears shall reap in joy.
PSALM 126:5 KJV

Then they cried out to the LORD in their trouble,
and He saved them out of their distresses.
PSALM 107:13 NKJV

A TIMELY TIP

When you're discouraged, disappointed, or hurt, don't spend too much time asking, "Why me, Lord?" Instead, ask, "What now, Lord?" and then get busy. When you do, you'll feel much better.

26

DISCIPLESHIP

"Follow Me," Jesus told them, "and I will make you fish for people!" Immediately they left their nets and followed Him.
MARK 1:17–18 HCSB

Jesus instructed His disciples to take up their cross and follow Him. His disciples must have known exactly what the Master meant. In Christ's day, prisoners were forced to carry their own crosses to the location where they would be put to death. So the message was clear: in order to follow Him, the disciples must deny themselves and, instead, trust Him completely. Nothing has changed since then.

If we are to be disciples of Christ, we must put Him first in our thoughts and our lives. Jesus never comes "next." He is always first. The paradox, of course, is that only by sacrificing ourselves to Him do we gain salvation for ourselves.

Do you want to be a worthy disciple of Christ? Then pick up your cross today, tomorrow, and every day that you live. When you do, He will bless you today, tomorrow, and forever.

When Jesus put the little child in the midst of His disciples,
He did not tell the little child to become like His disciples;
He told the disciples to become like the little child.

RUTH BELL GRAHAM

You cannot cooperate with Jesus in becoming what
He wants you to become and simultaneously be
what the world desires to make you. If you would say,
"Take the world but give me Jesus," then you must deny yourself
and take up your cross. The simple truth is that your "self"
must be put to death in order for you to get to the point where
for you to live is Christ. What will it be? The world and you,
or Jesus and you? You do have a choice to make.

KAY ARTHUR

If we just give God the little that we have,
we can trust Him to make it go around.

GLORIA GAITHER

Discipleship usually brings us into the necessity
of choice between duty and desire.

ELISABETH ELLIOT

Be filled with the Holy Spirit; join a church where
the members believe the Bible and know the Lord;
seek the fellowship of other Christians; learn and be
nourished by God's Word and His many promises.
Conversion is not the end of your journey.

CORRIE TEN BOOM

More from God's Word

For whoever wants to save his life will lose it, but whoever loses his life because of Me and the gospel will save it.
MARK 8:35 HCSB

Be imitators of God, therefore, as dearly loved children.
EPHESIANS 5:1 NIV

How happy is everyone who fears the LORD,
who walks in His ways!
PSALM 128:1 HCSB

Then Jesus spoke to them again:
"I am the light of the world. Anyone who follows Me will
never walk in the darkness but will have the light of life."
JOHN 8:12 HCSB

Whoever wants to be my disciple must deny themselves
and take up their cross and follow me.
MARK 8:34 NIV

A Timely Tip

Jesus has invited you to become His disciple. If you accept His invitation—and if you obey His commandments—you will be protected and blessed.

27

DISCIPLINE

Discipline yourself for the purpose of godliness.
1 TIMOTHY 4:7 NASB

It's not enough to preach the fine art of discipline; we must also live disciplined lives. Otherwise, our actions speak so loudly that our words become meaningless.

God does not reward apathy, laziness, or idleness, nor does He reward undisciplined behavior. Our heavenly Father has a way of helping those who first help themselves, and He expects us to lead disciplined lives despite worldly temptations to do otherwise.

The media glorifies leisure. The ultimate goal, so the message goes, is to win the lottery and then retire to some sunny paradise in order to while away the hours sitting idly by watching the waves splash onto the sand. Such leisure activities are fine for a few days, but not for a lifetime.

Life's greatest rewards are seldom the result of luck. More often than not, our greatest accomplishments require plenty of preparation and lots of work, which is perfectly fine with God. After all, He knows that we can do the work, and He knows the rewards that we'll earn when we finish the job. Besides, God knows that He will always help us complete the tasks He has set before us. As a matter of fact, God usually does at least half the work: the second half.

*Personal discipline is a most powerful character quality
and one worthy of dedicating your life to nurturing.*
ELIZABETH GEORGE

*Discipline, for the Christian, begins with the body.
We have only one. It is this body that is the primary
material given to us for sacrifice. We cannot give
our hearts to God and keep our bodies for ourselves.*
ELISABETH ELLIOT

*Working in the vineyard,
Working all the day,
Never be discouraged,
Only watch and pray.*
FANNY CROSBY

*Character is doing what you don't want to do
but know you should do.*
JOYCE MEYER

*God has given you special talents—
now it's your turn to give them back to God.*
MARIE T. FREEMAN

More from God's Word

Whatever you do, do your work heartily,
as for the Lord rather than for men.
COLOSSIANS 3:23 NASB

But the fruit of the Spirit is love, joy, peace,
patience, kindness, goodness, faith, gentleness, self-control.
Against such things there is no law.
GALATIANS 5:22–23 HCSB

Better to be patient than powerful;
better to have self-control than to conquer a city.
PROVERBS 16:32 NLT

Finishing is better than starting.
Patience is better than pride.
ECCLESIASTES 7:8 NLT

A final word: Be strong in the Lord and in his mighty power.
EPHESIANS 6:10 NLT

A Timely Tip

When you take a disciplined approach to your life and your responsibilities, God will reward your good judgment. Self-discipline pays—it always has and it always will.

28

ENCOURAGEMENT

But encourage each other daily, while it is still called today,
so that none of you is hardened by sin's deception.
HEBREWS 3:13 HCSB

Whether we realize it or not, all of us need encouragement. The world can be a difficult place, a place where we encounter the inevitable disappointments that are woven into the fabric of everyday life. So we all need boosters who are ready, willing, and able to cheer us on when times get tough.

God's Word teaches that we must treat others as we ourselves wish to be treated. Since we desire encouragement for ourselves, we should be quick to share it with others.

Whom will you encourage today? How many times will you share a smile, or a kind word, or a pat on the back? You'll probably have many opportunities to share the gift of encouragement. When you seize those opportunities, others will be blessed, and you'll be blessed, too. But not necessarily in that order.

*The glory of friendship is not the outstretched hand,
or the kindly smile, or the joy of companionship.
It is the spiritual inspiration that comes to one
when he discovers that someone else believes in him
and is willing to trust him with his friendship.*

CORRIE TEN BOOM

*Words. Do you fully understand their power?
Can any of us really grasp the mighty force behind
the things we say? Do we stop and think before we speak,
considering the potency of the words we utter?*

JONI EARECKSON TADA

*Don't forget that a single sentence, spoken at the right moment,
can change somebody's whole perspective on life.
A little encouragement can go a long, long way.*

MARIE T. FREEMAN

*Once you loosen up, let yourself be who you are:
the wonderful, witty woman whom God will use
to encourage and uplift other people.*

BARBARA JOHNSON

*True friends will always lift you higher and challenge
you to walk in a manner pleasing to our Lord.*

LISA BEVERE

More from God's Word

*Let us think about each other and help each other
to show love and do good deeds.*
HEBREWS 10:24 ICB

*So encourage each other and give each other strength,
just as you are doing now.*
1 THESSALONIANS 5:11 NCV

Bear one another's burdens, and so fulfill the law of Christ.
GALATIANS 6:2 NKJV

*When you talk, do not say harmful things,
but say what people need—words that will help
others become stronger. Then what you say will
do good to those who listen to you.*
EPHESIANS 4:29 NCV

*Now we exhort you, brethren, warn those who are unruly,
comfort the fainthearted, uphold the weak, be patient with all.*
1 THESSALONIANS 5:14 NKJV

A Timely Tip

You can't lift other people up without lifting yourself up, too. The more encouragement you give, the more you'll receive in return.

29

ENTHUSIASM

Whatever you do, do it enthusiastically,
as something done for the Lord and not for men.
COLOSSIANS 3:23 HCSB

As a Christian, you have many reasons to be enthusiastic about your life, your opportunities, and your future. After all, your eternal destiny is secure. Christ died for your sins, and He wants you to experience life abundant and life eternal. So what's not to get excited about?

Are you a passionate person and an enthusiastic Christian? Are you genuinely excited about your faith, your family, and your future? Hopefully, you can answer these questions with a resounding yes. But if your passion for life has waned, it's time to slow down long enough to recharge your spiritual batteries and reorder your priorities.

Each new day is an opportunity to put God first and celebrate His creation. Today, take time to count your blessings and take stock of your opportunities. And while you're at it, ask God for strength. When you sincerely petition Him, He will give you everything you need to live enthusiastically and abundantly.

Enthusiasm, like the flu, is contagious—
we get it from one another.
BARBARA JOHNSON

When the dream of our heart is one that God has planted there,
a strange happiness flows into us. At that moment, all of the
spiritual resources of the universe are released to help us.
Our praying is then at one with the will of God and becomes
a channel for the Creator's purposes for us and our world.
CATHERINE MARSHALL

Developing a positive attitude means working
continually to find what is uplifting and encouraging.
BARBARA JOHNSON

Your attitude toward others, work, and your daily life
is a reflection of your attitude toward God.
ELIZABETH GEORGE

It's ironic that one of the best remedies for impending
burnout is to give yourself away—to pick out one time
and place each week where you can stretch out your hands
for the pure joy of doing it.
LIZ CURTIS HIGGS

More from God's Word

Do your work with enthusiasm. Work as if you were serving the Lord, not as if you were serving only men and women.
EPHESIANS 6:7 NCV

But as for me, I will hope continually, and will praise You yet more and more.
PSALM 71:14 NASB

A happy heart makes the face cheerful, but heartache crushes the spirit.
PROVERBS 15:13 NIV

Rejoice always! Pray constantly. Give thanks in everything, for this is God's will for you in Christ Jesus.
1 THESSALONIANS 5:16–18 HCSB

Let the hearts of those who seek the LORD rejoice. Look to the LORD and his strength; seek his face always.
1 CHRONICLES 16:10–11 NIV

A Timely Tip

Today, as you interact with family, friends, and coworkers, share your courage, your hopes, your dreams, and your enthusiasm. Your positive outlook will be almost as big a blessing to them as it is to you.

30

ETERNAL LIFE

For God so loved the world, that he gave his only
begotten Son, that whosoever believeth in him
should not perish, but have everlasting life.

JOHN 3:16 KJV

Jesus is not only the light of the world; He is also its salvation. He came to this earth so that we might not perish, but instead spend eternity with Him. What a glorious gift; what a priceless opportunity.

As mere mortals, we cannot fully understand the scope, and thus the value, of eternal life. Our vision is limited but God's is not. He sees all things; He knows all things; and His plans for you extend throughout eternity.

If you haven't already done so, this moment is the perfect moment to turn your life over to God's only begotten son. When you give your heart to the Son, you belong to the Father—today, tomorrow, and for all eternity.

*Your choice to either receive or reject the Lord Jesus Christ
will determine where you spend eternity.*
ANNE GRAHAM LOTZ

*If you are a believer, your judgment will not determine your
eternal destiny. Christ's finished work on Calvary was applied
to you the moment you accepted Christ as Savior.*
BETH MOORE

*I can still hardly believe it. I, with shriveled, bent fingers,
atrophied muscles, gnarled knees, and no feeling from
the shoulders down, will one day have a new body—light,
bright, and clothed in righteousness—powerful and dazzling.*
JONI EARECKSON TADA

*God has promised us abundance, peace, and eternal life.
These treasures are ours for the asking; all we must do is claim
them. One of the great mysteries of life is why on earth do
so many of us wait so very long to lay claim to God's gifts?*
MARIE T. FREEMAN

*Like a shadow declining swiftly…away…like the dew
of the morning gone with the heat of the day; like the wind
in the treetops, like a wave of the sea, so are our lives
on earth when seen in light of eternity.*
RUTH BELL GRAHAM

More from God's Word

*I assure you: Anyone who hears My word and believes Him
who sent Me has eternal life and will not come under
judgment, but has passed from death to life.*
John 5:24 HCSB

*I have written these things to you who believe
in the name of the Son of God, so that you may know
that you have eternal life.*
1 John 5:13 HCSB

*For the wages of sin is death, but the gift of God
is eternal life in Christ Jesus our Lord.*
Romans 6:23 NIV

*The world and its desires pass away, but the man
who does the will of God lives forever.*
1 John 2:17 NIV

The last enemy that will be destroyed is death.
1 Corinthians 15:26 NKJV

A Timely Tip

God offers you the priceless gift of eternal life. If you have not
accepted His gift, the appropriate moment to do so is now.

31
EVIL

Be sober, be vigilant; because your adversary the devil walks about like a roaring lion, seeking whom he may devour.
1 PETER 5:8 NKJV

This world is God's creation, and it contains the wonderful fruits of His handiwork. But the world also contains countless opportunities to stray from God's will. Temptations are everywhere, and the devil, it seems, never takes a day off. Our task, as believers, is to turn away from temptation and to place our lives squarely in the center of God's will.

Evil is abroad in the world, and Satan continues to sow the seeds of destruction far and wide. In a very real sense, our world is at war: good versus evil, sin versus righteousness, hope versus suffering, praise versus apathy. As Christians, we must ensure that we place ourselves squarely on the right side of these conflicts: God's side. How can we do it? By thoughtfully studying God's Word, by regularly worshiping with fellow believers, and by guarding our hearts and minds against the subtle temptations of the enemy. When we do, we are protected.

Are you determined to stand up against evil whenever and wherever you confront it? And are you fully prepared to distance yourself from the countless temptations that have become so thoroughly woven into the fabric of society? If so, congratulations. That means you're an active-duty participant in the battle against a powerful and dangerous adversary. And with God's help, you're destined to win the battle *and* the war.

There are two great forces at work in the world today:
the unlimited power of God and the limited power of Satan.
CORRIE TEN BOOM

We are in a continual battle with the spiritual forces of evil,
but we will triumph when we yield to God's leading
and call on His powerful presence in prayer.
SHIRLEY DOBSON

Where God's ministers are most successful, there the powers
of darkness marshal their forces for the conflict.
LOTTIE MOON

Holiness has never been the driving force
of the majority. It is, however, mandatory for anyone
who wants to enter the kingdom.
ELISABETH ELLIOT

Light is stronger than darkness—
darkness cannot "comprehend" or "overcome" it.
ANNE GRAHAM LOTZ

More from God's Word

Put on the full armor of God so that you can stand against the tactics of the Devil.
Ephesians 6:11 HCSB

Don't fear those who kill the body but are not able to kill the soul; but rather, fear Him who is able to destroy both soul and body in hell.
Matthew 10:28 HCSB

Therefore submit to God. Resist the devil and he will flee from you. Draw near to God and He will draw near to you. Cleanse your hands, you sinners; and purify your hearts, you double-minded.
James 4:7–8 NKJV

Dear friend, do not imitate what is evil, but what is good. The one who does good is of God; the one who does evil has not seen God.
3 John 1:11 HCSB

The house of the wicked shall be overthrown: but the tabernacle of the upright shall flourish.
Proverbs 14:11 KJV

A Timely Tip

Evil exists somewhere very near you. Because you live in a temptation-filled world, you must guard your eyes, your thoughts, and your heart—all day, every day.

32
Faith

For truly I say to you, if you have faith as a mustard seed,
you shall say to this mountain, "Move from here to there,"
and it will move; and nothing will be impossible to you.
MATTHEW 17:20 NASB

The Bible makes it clear: faith is powerful. With it, we can move mountains. With it, we can endure any hardship. With it, we can rise above the challenges of everyday life and live victoriously, whatever our circumstances.

Is your faith strong enough to move the mountains in your own life? If so, you're already tapped in to a source of strength that never fails: God's strength. But if your spiritual batteries are in need of recharging, don't be discouraged. God's strength is always available to those who seek it.

The first element of a successful life is faith: faith in God, faith in His promises, and faith in His Son. When our faith in the Creator is strong, we can then have faith in ourselves, knowing that we are tools in the hands of a loving God who made mountains— and moves them—according to a perfect plan that only He can see.

Faith does not concern itself with the entire journey.
One step is enough.
LETTIE COWMAN

Grace calls you to get up, throw off your blanket
of helplessness, and to move on through life in faith.
KAY ARTHUR

Just as our faith strengthens our prayer life,
so do our prayers deepen our faith. Let us pray often,
starting today, for a deeper, more powerful faith.
SHIRLEY DOBSON

Faith does not concern itself
with the entire journey.
One step is enough.
LETTIE COWMAN

If God chooses to remain silent, faith is content.
RUTH BELL GRAHAM

More from God's Word

Don't be afraid, because I am your God.
I will make you strong and will help you;
I will support you with my right hand that saves you.
ISAIAH 41:10 NCV

Blessed are they that have not seen,
and yet have believed.
JOHN 20:29 KJV

Don't be afraid. Only believe.
MARK 5:36 HCSB

All things are possible for the one who believes.
MARK 9:23 NCV

And he said unto her, Daughter, thy faith hath
made thee whole; go in peace, and be whole.
MARK 5:34 KJV

A Timely Tip

If your faith is strong enough, you and God—working together—can move mountains. No challenge is too big for God.

33

FAITHFULNESS

He who follows righteousness and mercy finds life,
righteousness, and honor.
PROVERBS 21:21 NKJV

When we are faithful to God, and when we place Him at the center of our lives, every day is a cause for celebration. The Lord fills each day to the brim with possibilities, and He challenges us to use our lives for His purposes.

Every day, you are faced with choices, more choices than you can count. You can do the right thing, or not. You can be prudent, or not. You can be kind, and generous, and obedient to God. Or not.

Today, the world will offer you countless opportunities to demonstrate your faithfulness. But you will also be tempted to let down your guard and, by doing so, make needless mistakes that may injure yourself or your loved ones. So be watchful and obedient. Guard your heart by giving it to your heavenly Father; it is safe with Him.

Faithfulness today is the best preparation
for the demands of tomorrow.
ELISABETH ELLIOT

Determination and faithfulness are the nails
used to build the house of God's dreams.
BARBARA JOHNSON

Success isn't the key. Faithfulness is.
JONI EARECKSON TADA

Our faithfulness, or lack of it,
will have an overwhelming impact
on the heritage of our children.
BETH MOORE

I am more and more persuaded
that all that is required of us is faithful seed-sowing.
The harvest is bound to follow.
ANNIE ARMSTRONG

More from God's Word

*But seek first the kingdom of God and His righteousness,
and all these things will be provided for you.*
MATTHEW 6:33 HCSB

*Those who love Your law have great peace,
and nothing causes them to stumble.*
PSALM 119:165 NASB

*Be joyful in hope, patient in affliction,
faithful in prayer.*
ROMANS 12:12 NIV

Therefore let everyone who is faithful pray to You.
PSALM 32:6 HCSB

*Therefore everyone who hears these words
of mine and puts them into practice is like
a wise man who built his house on the rock.*
MATHEW 7:24–25 NIV

A Timely Tip

Because God is just, He rewards good behavior just as surely as He punishes sin. Obedience earns God's pleasure; disobedience doesn't.

34

FAMILY

Choose for yourselves this day whom you will serve . . . .
But as for me and my house, we will serve the LORD.
JOSHUA 24:15 NKJV

A happy home is a treasure from God. If the Lord has blessed you
with a close-knit family and a peaceful home, give thanks to your
Creator because He has given you one of His most precious earthly
possessions.

You inhabit a demanding world, a place where life can be tough
and pressures can be intense. Even when the demands of everyday
life are great, you must never forget that you have been entrusted
with a profound responsibility: the responsibility of contributing to
your family's emotional and spiritual health. It's a big job, but with
the Lord's help, you can do it.

So the next time your home life becomes stressful, remember
that your loved ones are a gift from above. You should praise God
for that gift—and you should act accordingly.

For whatever life holds for you and your family
in the coming days, weave the unfailing fabric
of God's Word through your heart and mind.
It will hold strong, even if the rest of life unravels.

GIGI GRAHAM TCHIVIDJIAN

One way or the other, God, who thought up the family in
the first place, has the very best idea of how to bring sense to
the chaos of broken relationships we see all around us. I really
believe that if I remain still and listen a lot, He will share
some solutions with me so I can share them with others.

JILL BRISCOE

When God asks someone to do something for Him entailing
sacrifice, he makes up for it in surprising ways. Though He
has led Bill all over the world to preach the gospel, He has not
forgotten the little family in the mountains of North Carolina.

RUTH BELL GRAHAM

Living life with a consistent spiritual walk
deeply influences those we love most.

VONETTE BRIGHT

I think the greatest benefit to having a big family,
especially a family with five or more children,
is that it's harder to be selfish. In today's prosperous world,
it's hard to teach our children sacrifice.

LISA WHELCHEL

More from God's Word

*Every kingdom divided against itself is headed for destruction,
and a house divided against itself falls.*
LUKE 11:17 HCSB

*Better a dry crust with peace than a house
full of feasting with strife.*
PROVERBS 17:1 HCSB

*But if anyone does not provide for his own,
and especially for those of his household,
he has denied the faith and is worse than an unbeliever.*
1 TIMOTHY 5:8 NASB

*Their first responsibility is to show godliness at home
and repay their parents by taking care of them.
This is something that pleases God.*
1 TIMOTHY 5:4 NLT

*But now faith, hope, love, abide these three;
but the greatest of these is love.*
1 CORINTHIANS 13:13 NASB

A Timely Tip

If you're lucky enough to be a member of a loving, supportive family, then you owe it to yourself—and to them—to share your thoughts, your hopes, your encouragement, and your love.

35
FEAR

Peace I leave with you; My peace I give to you;
not as the world gives do I give to you.
Do not let your heart be troubled, nor let it be fearful.
JOHN 14:27 NASB

All of us may find our courage tested by the inevitable disappointments and tragedies of life. After all, ours is a world filled with uncertainty, hardship, sickness, and danger. Old Man Trouble, it seems, is never too far from the front door.

When we focus upon our fears and our doubts, we may find many reasons to lie awake at night and fret about the uncertainties of the coming day. A better strategy, of course, is to focus not upon our fears but instead upon our God.

God is as near as your next breath, and He is in control. He offers salvation to all His children, including you. God is your shield and your strength; you are His forever. So don't focus your thoughts upon the fears of the day. Instead, trust God's plan and His eternal love for you. And remember: God is good, and He has the last word.

I have found the perfect antidote for fear.
Whenever it sticks up its ugly face, I clobber it with prayer.
DALE EVANS ROGERS

Our lives are full of supposes. Suppose this should happen,
or suppose that should happen; what could we do; how could
we bear it? But, if we are living in the dwelling place of God,
all these supposes vanish and we shall be free from fear.
HANNAH WHITALL SMITH

The heart set to do the Father's
will need never fear defeat.
ELISABETH ELLIOT

When once we are assured that God is good,
then there can be nothing left to fear.
HANNAH WHITALL SMITH

His hand on me is a father's hand,
gently guiding and encouraging.
His hand lets me know He is with me,
so I am not afraid.
MARY MORRISON SUGGS

More from God's Word

But He said to them, "It is I; do not be afraid."
JOHN 6:20 NKJV

The LORD is my light and my salvation—
whom should I fear? The LORD is the stronghold of my life—
of whom should I be afraid?
PSALM 27:1 HCSB

Fear not, for I am with you; be not dismayed,
for I am your God. I will strengthen you, yes, I will help you,
I will uphold you with My righteous right hand.
ISAIAH 41:10 NKJV

Even though I walk through the valley of the shadow of death,
I will fear no evil, for you are with me;
your rod and your staff, they comfort me.
PSALM 23:4 NIV

Be not afraid, only believe.
MARK 5:36 KJV

A Timely Tip

Are you feeling anxious or fearful? If so, trust God to handle those problems that are simply too big for you to solve. Entrust the future—your future—to God.

36

FEAR OF GOD

The fear of the LORD is the beginning of knowledge,
but fools despise wisdom and instruction.

PROVERBS 1:7 NKJV

Do you have a healthy, fearful respect for God's power? If so, you are both wise and obedient. And, because you are a thoughtful believer, you also understand that genuine wisdom begins with a profound appreciation for God's limitless power.

God praises humility and punishes pride. That's why God's greatest servants will always be those humble men and women who care less for their own glory and more for God's glory. In God's kingdom, the only way to achieve greatness is to shun it. And the only way to be wise is to understand these facts: God is great; He is all-knowing; and He is all-powerful. We must respect Him, and we must humbly obey His commandments, or we must accept the consequences of our misplaced pride.

If a person fears God, he or she has no reason
to fear anything else. On the other hand,
if a person does not fear God, then fear becomes a way of life.
BETH MOORE

The center of God's will is our only safety.
BETSIE TEN BOOM

God is God. Because He is God, He is worthy
of my trust and obedience. I will find rest nowhere
but in His holy will, a will that is unspeakably beyond
my largest notions of what He is up to.
ELISABETH ELLIOT

An ongoing relationship with God through His Word
is essential to the Christian's consistent victory.
BETH MOORE

Look upon your chastening as God's chariots
sent to carry your soul into the high places
of spiritual achievement.
HANNAH WHITALL SMITH

More from God's Word

When all has been heard, the conclusion of the matter is: fear God and keep His commands.
ECCLESIASTES 12:13 HCSB

The fear of the LORD is a fountain of life.
PROVERBS 14:27 NKJV

You shall walk after the LORD your God and fear Him, and keep His commandments and obey His voice, and you shall serve Him and hold fast to Him.
DEUTERONOMY 13:4 NKJV

Respect for the LORD will teach you wisdom. If you want to be honored, you must be humble.
PROVERBS 15:33 NCV

Honor all men. Love the brotherhood. Fear God. Honor the king.
1 PETER 2:17 KJV

A Timely Tip

When you possess a healthy fear of God, He will guide your steps and guard your heart.

37
FELLOWSHIP

Love one another fervently with a pure heart.
1 PETER 1:22 NKJV

God's Word teaches us about the importance of Christian fellowship. The Lord doesn't intend for us to be solitary believers. He wants us to join together as we worship Him and serve His children.

Your association with fellow Christians should be uplifting, encouraging, enlightening, and consistent. In short, fellowship with other believers should be an integral part of your everyday life.

Are you an active member of your own fellowship? Are you a builder of bridges inside the four walls of your church and outside it? Do you contribute to God's glory by contributing your time and your talents to a close-knit band of believers? Hopefully so. The fellowship of believers is intended to be a powerful tool for spreading God's Good News and uplifting His children. And the Lord intends for you to be a fully contributing member of that fellowship. Your intentions should be the same.

Be united with other Christians. A wall with loose bricks
is not good. The bricks must be cemented together.
CORRIE TEN BOOM

Only when we realize that we are indeed broken,
that we are not independent, that we cannot do it ourselves,
can we turn to God and take that which He has given us,
no matter what it is, and create with it.
MADELEINE L'ENGLE

In God's economy you will be hard-pressed to find many
examples of successful "Lone Rangers."
LUCI SWINDOLL

It is wonderful to have all kinds of human support systems,
but we must always stand firm in God and in Him alone.
JOYCE MEYER

One of the ways God refills us after failure is through
the blessing of Christian fellowship. Just experiencing
the joy of simple activities shared with other children
of God can have a healing effect on us.
ANNE GRAHAM LOTZ

More from God's Word

Now I urge you, brothers, in the name of our Lord Jesus Christ, that you all say the same thing, that there be no divisions among you, and that you be united with the same understanding and the same conviction.
1 CORINTHIANS 1:10 HCSB

It is good and pleasant when God's people live together in peace!
PSALM 133:1 NCV

Beyond all these things put on love, which is the perfect bond of unity.
COLOSSIANS 3:14 NASB

Accept each other just as Christ has accepted you so that God will be given glory.
ROMANS 15:7 NLT

The one who loves his brother remains in the light, and there is no cause for stumbling in him.
1 JOHN 2:10 HCSB

A Timely Tip

You need fellowship with men and women of faith. And your Christian friends need fellowship with you. God intends for you to be an active member of your church, and your intentions should be the same.

38

FOLLOWING CHRIST

Then He said to them all, "If anyone wants to come with Me,
he must deny himself, take up his cross daily, and follow Me."
LUKE 9:23 HCSB

Every day, we're presented with countless opportunities to honor God by following in the footsteps of His Son. But we're sorely tempted to do otherwise. The world is filled to the brim with temptations and distractions that beckon us down a different path.

Elisabeth Elliot had this advice for believers everywhere: "Choose Jesus Christ! Deny yourself, take up the Cross, and follow Him, for the world must be shown. The world must see, in us, a discernible, visible, startling difference."

Today, do your part to take up the cross and follow Him, even if the world encourages you to do otherwise. When you're traveling step-by-step with the Son of God, you're always on the right path.

*Think of this—we may live together with Him here and now,
a daily walking with Him who loved us and gave Himself for us.*
ELISABETH ELLIOT

*Will you, with a glad and eager surrender, hand yourself and all
that concerns you over into His hands? If you will do this, your soul
will begin to know something of the joy of union with Christ.*
HANNAH WHITALL SMITH

*The Christian faith is meant to be lived moment by moment.
It isn't some broad, general outline—it's a long walk with
a real Person. Details count: passing thoughts, small sacrifices,
a few encouraging words, little acts of kindness,
brief victories over nagging sins.*
JONI EARECKSON TADA

*You cannot cooperate with Jesus in becoming what He wants you
to become and simultaneously be what the world desires to make
you. If you would say, "Take the world but give me Jesus," then
you must deny yourself and take up your cross. The simple truth
is that your "self" must be put to death in order for you to get to
the point where for you to live is Christ. What will it be? The
world and you, or Jesus and you? You do have a choice to make.*
KAY ARTHUR

*O, that I could consecrate myself, soul and body, to His service
forever; O, that I could give myself up to Him, so as never
more to attempt to be my own or to have any will or affection
improper for those conformed to Him.*
LOTTIE MOON

More from God's Word

But whoever keeps His word, truly in him the love of God is perfected. This is how we know we are in Him: the one who says he remains in Him should walk just as He walked.
1 John 2:5–6 HCSB

For we walk by faith, not by sight.
2 Corinthians 5:7 HCSB

Walk in a manner worthy of the God who calls you into His own kingdom and glory.
1 Thessalonians 2:12 NASB

Take my yoke upon you, and learn of me; for I am meek and lowly in heart: and ye shall find rest unto your souls. For my yoke is easy, and my burden is light.
Matthew 11:29–30 KJV

Whoever is not willing to carry the cross and follow me is not worthy of me. Those who try to hold on to their lives will give up true life. Those who give up their lives for me will hold on to true life.
Matthew 10:38–39 NCV

A Timely Tip

Think about your relationship with Jesus: what it is, and what it can be. Then, as you embark upon the next phase of your life's journey, be sure to walk with your Savior every step of the way.

39

FORGIVENESS

Judge not, and you shall not be judged. Condemn not, and you shall not be condemned. Forgive, and you will be forgiven.
LUKE 6:37 NKJV

There's no doubt about it: forgiveness is difficult. Being frail, fallible, imperfect human beings, we are quick to anger, quick to blame, slow to forgive, and even slower to forget. Yet as Christians, we are commanded to forgive others, just as we, too, have been forgiven. So even when forgiveness is difficult, we must ask God to help us move beyond the spiritual stumbling blocks of bitterness and hate.

If, in your heart, you hold bitterness against even a single person, forgive. If there exists even one person, alive or dead, whom you have not forgiven, follow God's commandment and His will for your life: forgive. If you are embittered against yourself for some past mistake or shortcoming, forgive. Then, to the best of your abilities, forget. And move on. Bitterness and regret are not part of God's plan for your life. Forgiveness is.

*Forgiveness is the key that unlocks the door of resentment
and the handcuffs of hate. It is the power that breaks
the chains of bitterness and the shackles of selfishness.*

CORRIE TEN BOOM

*Forgiveness is the economy of the heart.
Forgiveness saves the expense of anger,
the cost of hatred, the waste of spirits.*

HANNAH MORE

*God expects us to forgive others as He has forgiven us;
we are to follow His example by having a forgiving heart.*

VONETTE BRIGHT

*Forgiveness is actually the best revenge
because it not only sets us free from the person we forgive,
but it frees us to move into all that God has in store for us.*

STORMIE OMARTIAN

*The more you practice the art of forgiving,
the quicker you'll master the art of living.*

MARIE T. FREEMAN

More from God's Word

Above all, love each other deeply,
because love covers over a multitude of sins.
1 Peter 4:8 NIV

And be kind to one another,
tenderhearted, forgiving one another,
just as God in Christ forgave you.
Ephesians 4:32 NKJV

But I say to you, love your enemies,
and pray for those who persecute you.
Matthew 5:44 NASB

And whenever you stand praying,
if you have anything against anyone, forgive him,
so that your Father in heaven
may also forgive you your wrongdoing.
Mark 11:25 HCSB

Blessed are the merciful,
for they will be shown mercy.
Matthew 5:7 NIV

A Timely Tip

Forgiveness is its own reward. Bitterness is its own punishment.
Guard your words and thoughts accordingly.

40
FRIENDS

A friend loves at all times, and a brother is born for adversity.
PROVERBS 17:17 NIV

Our friends are gifts from above. God places them along our path and asks us to treat them with kindness, love, and respect. His Word teaches us that true friendship is both a blessing and a treasure.

Emily Dickinson spoke for friends everywhere when she observed, "My friends are my estate." Dickinson understood that friends are among our most treasured possessions. But unlike a bank account or a stock certificate, the value of a true friendship is beyond measure.

Today, celebrate the joys of building and preserving your personal estate of lifelong friends. Give thanks for the laughter, the loyalty, the sharing, and the trust. And while you're at it, take the time to reconnect with a long-lost friend. When you do, you will have increased two personal fortunes at once.

We long to find someone who has been where we've been,
who shares our fragile skies, who sees our sunsets
with the same shades of blue.
BETH MOORE

Inasmuch as anyone pushes you nearer to God,
he or she is your friend.
BARBARA JOHNSON

You could have been born in another time
and another place, but God determined to "people"
your life with these particular friends.
JONI EARECKSON TADA

The best times in life are made a thousand
times better when shared with a dear friend.
LUCI SWINDOLL

Friends are like a quilt with lots of different shapes,
sizes, colors, and patterns of fabric. But the end result
brings you warmth and comfort in a support system
that makes you life richer and fuller.
SUZANNE DALE EZELL

More from God's Word

As iron sharpens iron, so people can improve each other.
PROVERBS 27:17 NCV

*It is good and pleasant when
God's people live together in peace!*
PSALM 133:1 NCV

*Oil and incense bring joy to the heart,
and the sweetness of a friend is better than self-counsel.*
PROVERBS 27:9 HCSB

*Dear friends, if God loved us in this way,
we also must love one another.*
1 JOHN 4:11 HCSB

Thine own friend, and thy father's friend, forsake not.
PROVERBS 27:10 KJV

A Timely Tip

The best rule for making and keeping friends is, not surprisingly, the golden one. To have good friends, be a good friend.

41

FUTURE

There is surely a future hope for you,
and your hope will not be cut off.
PROVERBS 23:18 NIV

If you've entrusted your heart to Christ, your eternal fate is secure and your future is eternally bright. No matter how troublesome your present circumstances may seem, you need not fear because the Lord has promised that you are His now and forever.

Of course, you won't be exempt from the normal challenges of life here on earth. While you're here, you'll probably experience your fair share of disappointments, emergencies, setbacks, and outright failures. But these are only temporary defeats.

Are you willing to place your future in the hands of a loving and all-knowing God? Do you trust in the ultimate goodness of His plan for you? Will you face today's challenges with hope and optimism? You should. After all, God created you for a very important purpose: His purpose. And you still have important work to do: His work. So today, as you live in the present and look to the future, remember that God has a marvelous plan for you. Act—and believe—accordingly.

You can look forward with hope,
because one day there will be no more separation,
no more scars, and no more suffering in My Father's House.
It's the home of your dreams!
ANNE GRAHAM LOTZ

The future lies all before us. Shall it only be a slight advance
upon what we usually do? Ought it not to be a bound,
a leap forward to altitudes of endeavor
and success undreamed of before?
ANNIE ARMSTRONG

Our future may look fearfully intimidating,
yet we can look up to the Engineer of the Universe,
confident that nothing escapes His attention
or slips out of the control of those strong hands.
ELISABETH ELLIOT

Allow your dreams a place in your prayers and plans.
God-given dreams can help you move
into the future He is preparing for you.
BARBARA JOHNSON

Every experience God gives us, every person
He brings into our lives, is the perfect preparation
for the future that only He can see.
CORRIE TEN BOOM

More from God's Word

For I know the thoughts that I think toward you,
says the LORD, thoughts of peace and not of evil,
to give you a future and a hope. Then you will call upon Me
and go and pray to Me, and I will listen to you.
JEREMIAH 29:11–12 NKJV

But if we look forward to something we don't yet have,
we must wait patiently and confidently.
ROMANS 8:25 NLT

The LORD is my light and my salvation—
whom should I fear? The LORD is the stronghold of my life—
of whom should I be afraid?
PSALM 27:1 HCSB

Wisdom is pleasing to you. If you find it,
you have hope for the future.
PROVERBS 24:14 NCV

Rest in God alone, my soul, for my hope comes from Him.
PSALM 62:5 HCSB

A Timely Tip

Hope for the future is simply one aspect of trusting God. When you seek God's guidance in every aspect of your life, your future is secure.

42
GENEROSITY

Freely you have received; freely give.
MATTHEW 10:8 NIV

The theme of generosity is woven into the fabric of God's Word. Our Creator instructs us to give generously—and cheerfully—to those in need. And He promises that when we do give of our time, our talents, and our resources, we will be blessed.

Jesus was the perfect example of generosity. He gave us everything, even His earthly life, so that we, His followers, might receive abundance, peace, and eternal life. He was always generous, always kind, always willing to help "the least of these." And, if we are to follow in His footsteps, we, too, must be generous.

Sometime today, you'll encounter someone who needs a helping hand or a word of encouragement. When you encounter a person in need, think of yourself as Christ's ambassador. And remember that whatever you do for the least of these, you also do for Him.

The goodness you receive from God
is a treasure for you to share with others.
ELIZABETH GEORGE

No matter how little you have,
you can always give some of it away.
CATHERINE MARSHALL

As faithful stewards of what we have, ought we not
to give earnest thought to our staggering surplus?
ELISABETH ELLIOT

Why should we not, instead of the paltry offerings
we make, do something that will prove that we are
really in earnest in claiming to be followers of Him who,
though He was rich, for our sake became poor?
LOTTIE MOON

You can always give without loving,
but you can never love without giving.
AMY CARMICHAEL

More from God's Word

So let each one give as he purposes in his heart,
not grudgingly or of necessity; for God loves a cheerful giver.
2 Corinthians 9:7 NKJV

If you have two shirts, give one to the poor.
If you have food, share it with those who are hungry.
Luke 3:11 NLT

You should remember the words of the Lord Jesus:
"It is more blessed to give than to receive."
Acts 20:35 NLT

Whenever we have the opportunity, we should do good to
everyone—especially to those in the family of faith.
Galatians 6:10 NLT

Truly I tell you, whatever you did for one of the least of these
brothers and sisters of mine, you did for me.
Matthew 25:40 NIV

A Timely Tip

There's a direct relationship between generosity and joy—the more you share with others, the more joy you'll experience for yourself.

43
GOD FIRST

You shall have no other gods before Me.
EXODUS 20:3 NKJV

For most of us, these are very busy times. We have obligations at home, at work, at school, on social media. From the moment we rise until we drift off to sleep at night, we have things to do and people to contact. So how do we find time for God? We must make time for Him, plain and simple. When we put God first, we're blessed. But when we succumb to the pressures and temptations of the world, we inevitably pay a price for our misguided priorities.

In the book of Exodus, God warns that we should put no gods before Him. Yet all too often, we place our Lord in second, third, or fourth place as we focus on other things. When we place our desires for possessions and status above our love for God— or when we yield to the countless distractions that surround us— we forfeit the peace that might otherwise be ours.

In the wilderness, Satan offered Jesus earthly power and unimaginable riches, but Jesus refused. Instead, He chose to worship His heavenly Father. We must do likewise by putting God first and worshiping Him only. God must come first. Always first.

Choose Jesus Christ! Deny yourself, take up the Cross, and follow Him, for the world must be shown. The world must see, in us, a discernible, visible, startling difference.

ELISABETH ELLIOT

If you are receiving your affirmation, love, self-worth, joy, strength, and acceptance from anywhere but God, He will shake it.

LISA BEVERE

Make God's will the focus of your life day by day. If you seek to please Him and Him alone, you'll find yourself satisfied with life.

KAY ARTHUR

The manifold rewards of a serious, consistent prayer life demonstrate clearly that time with our Lord should be our first priority.

SHIRLEY DOBSON

The most important thing you must decide to do every day is put the Lord first.

ELIZABETH GEORGE

More from God's Word

*Jesus said to him, "'You shall love the Lord your God with
all your heart, with all your soul, and with all your mind.'
This is the first and great commandment."*
MATTHEW 22:37–38 NKJV

*No one can serve two masters. For you will hate one
and love the other, or be devoted to one and despise the other.
You cannot serve God and be enslaved to money.*
LUKE 16:13 NLT

Be careful not to forget the LORD.
DEUTERONOMY 6:12 HCSB

*Do not love the world or the things that belong to the world.
If anyone loves the world, love for the Father is not in him.*
1 JOHN 2:15 HCSB

*With my whole heart I have sought You;
oh, let me not wander from Your commandments!*
PSALM 119:10 NKJV

A Timely Tip

As you establish priorities for your day and your life, God
deserves first place. And you deserve the experience of putting Him
there.

44

GOD'S CALLING

I urge you to live a life worthy of the calling you have received.
EPHESIANS 4:1 NIV

God created you on purpose. He has a plan for your life that only you, with your unique array of talents and your own particular set of circumstances, can fulfill. The Lord is calling you; He's gently guiding you to the place where you can accomplish the greatest good for yourself and for His kingdom.

Have you already heard God's call? And are you doing your best to pursue His plan for your life? If so, you're blessed. But if you have not yet discovered God's plan for your life, don't panic. There's still time to hear His call and to follow His path. To find that path, keep searching and keep praying. Answers will come.

The Creator has placed you in a particular location, amid particular people, with unique opportunities to serve. And He has given you all the tools you need to accomplish His plans. So listen for His voice, watch for His signs, and prepare yourself for the call—His call—that is certain to come.

*Only God's chosen task for you will ultimately satisfy.
Do not wait until it is too late to realize the privilege
of serving Him in His chosen position for you.*
BETH MOORE

*In the very place where God has put us, whatever its
limitations, whatever kind of work it may be,
we may indeed serve the Lord Christ.*
ELISABETH ELLIOT

*God will help us become the people we are meant to be,
if only we will ask Him.*
HANNAH WHITALL SMITH

*In the center of a hurricane there is absolute quiet and peace.
There is no safer place than in the center of the will of God.*
CORRIE TEN BOOM

*It's important that you keep asking God to show you what
He wants you to do. If you don't ask, you won't know.*
STORMIE OMARTIAN

More from God's Word

But as God has distributed to each one,
as the Lord has called each one, so let him walk.
1 Corinthians 7:17 NKJV

For whoever does the will of God is My brother
and My sister and mother.
Mark 3:35 NKJV

And we know that all things work together
for good to those who love God, to those who are
the called according to His purpose.
Romans 8:28 NKJV

For many are called, but few are chosen.
Matthew 22:14 KJV

For you have need of endurance, so that when you have
done the will of God, you may receive what was promised.
Hebrews 10:36 NASB

A Timely Tip

God has a plan for your life, a divine calling that only you can fulfill. How you choose to respond to His calling will determine the direction you take and the contributions you make.

45

GOD'S FORGIVENESS

If we confess our sins, He is faithful and righteous to forgive us
our sins and to cleanse us from all unrighteousness.
1 JOHN 1:9 NASB

The Bible promises us that God will forgive our sins if we ask Him. It's our duty to ask; when we've fulfilled that responsibility, He will always fulfill His promise. Yet many of us continue to punish ourselves—with needless guilt and self-loathing—for mistakes that our Creator has long since forgiven and forgotten (Isaiah 43:25).

If you haven't managed to forgive yourself for some past mistake, or for a series of poor decisions, it's time to rearrange your thinking. If God has forgiven you, how can you withhold forgiveness from yourself? The answer, of course, is that God's mercy is intended to wash your sins away. That's what the Lord wants, and if you're good enough for Him, you're good enough.

It doesn't matter how big the sin is or how small,
it doesn't matter whether it was spontaneous or malicious.
God will forgive you if you come to Him and confess your sin!
ANNE GRAHAM LOTZ

There is nothing that God cannot forgive except for
the rejection of Christ. No matter how black the sin, how
hideous the sin, if we but confess it to Him in true repentance
and faith, He will forgive. He will accept and forgive.
RUTH BELL GRAHAM

We cannot out-sin God's ability to forgive us.
BETH MOORE

God expects us to forgive others as He has forgiven us;
we are to follow His example by having a forgiving heart.
VONETTE BRIGHT

There is only One who can cleanse us
from our sins—He who made us.
CORRIE TEN BOOM

More from God's Word

*All the prophets testify about Him that through His name
everyone who believes in Him will receive forgiveness of sins.*
ACTS 10:43 HCSB

*But the mercy of the LORD is from everlasting
to everlasting upon them that fear him,
and his righteousness unto children's children.*
PSALM 103:17 KJV

*Let us, then, feel very sure that we can come
before God's throne where there is grace. There we can
receive mercy and grace to help us when we need it.*
HEBREWS 4:16 NCV

Be merciful, just as your Father is merciful.
LUKE 6:36 NIV

*It is I who sweep away your transgressions
for My own sake and remember your sins no more.*
ISAIAH 43:25 HCSB

A Timely Tip

You cannot do anything that God can't forgive. God forgives
sin when you ask . . . so ask! God stands ready to forgive. The next
move is yours.

46

GOD'S GUIDANCE

*Trust in the LORD with all your heart, and lean not
on your own understanding; in all your ways
acknowledge Him, and He shall direct your paths.*

PROVERBS 3:5–6 NKJV

When we ask for God's guidance, with our hearts and minds open to His direction, He will lead us along a path of His choosing. But for many of us, listening to God is hard. We have so many things we want, and so many needs to pray for, that we spend far more time talking at God than we do listening to Him.

Corrie ten Boom observed, "God's guidance is even more important than common sense. I can declare that the deepest darkness is outshone by the light of Jesus." These words remind us that life is best lived when we seek the Lord's direction early and often.

Our Father has many ways to make Himself known. Our challenge is to make ourselves open to His instruction. So, if you're unsure of your next step, trust God's promises and talk to Him often. When you do, He'll guide your steps today, tomorrow, and forever.

*Walk in the daylight of God's will because
then you will be safe; you will not stumble.*
ANNE GRAHAM LOTZ

*Are you serious about wanting God's guidance
to become a personal reality in your life?
The first step is to tell God that you know
you can't manage your own life; that you need His help.*
CATHERINE MARSHALL

*It is a joy that God never abandons His children.
He guides faithfully all who listen to His directions.*
CORRIE TEN BOOM

*Whether our fear is absolutely realistic
or out of proportion in our minds,
our greatest refuge is Jesus Christ.*
LUCI SWINDOLL

*Only believe, don't fear. Our Master, Jesus,
always watches over us, and no matter what
the persecution, Jesus will surely overcome it.*
LOTTIE MOON

More from God's Word

Yet LORD, You are our Father; we are the clay, and You are our potter; we all are the work of Your hands.
ISAIAH 64:8 HCSB

*Teach me to do Your will, for You are my God;
Your Spirit is good. Lead me in the land of uprightness.*
PSALM 143:10 NKJV

*The LORD says, "I will guide you along the best pathway
for your life. I will advise you and watch over you."*
PSALM 32:8 NLT

*Show me thy ways, O LORD; teach me thy paths.
Lead me in thy truth, and teach me: for thou art the God
of my salvation; on thee do I wait all the day.*
PSALM 25:4–5 KJV

*Morning by morning he wakens me and opens my
understanding to his will. The Sovereign LORD
has spoken to me, and I have listened.*
ISAIAH 50:4–5 NLT

A Timely Tip

If you want God's guidance, ask for it. When you pray for guidance, the Lord will give it. He will guide your steps if you let Him. Let Him.

47
GOD'S LOVE

And we have known and believed the love
that God has for us. God is love, and he who abides
in love abides in God, and God in him.

1 JOHN 4:16 NKJV

Make no mistake about it: God loves our world. He loves it so much, in fact, that He sent His only begotten Son to die for our sins. And now we, as believers, are challenged to return God's love by obeying His commandments and honoring His Son.

When you open your heart and accept God's love, you are transformed not just for today, but for all eternity. When you accept the Father's love, you feel differently about yourself, your world, your neighbors, your family, and your church. When you experience God's presence and invite His Son into your heart, you feel the need to share His message and to obey His commandments.

God loved this world so much that He sent His Son to save it. And now only one real question remains for you: what, friend, will you do in response to God's love? The answer should be obvious: If you haven't already done so, accept Jesus Christ as Your Savior. He's waiting patiently for you, but please don't make Him wait another minute longer.

God knows everything. He can manage everything,
and He loves us. Surely this is enough
for a fullness of joy that is beyond words.
HANNAH WHITALL SMITH

The fact is, God no longer deals with us in judgment
but in mercy. If people got what they deserved, this old planet
would have ripped apart at the seams centuries ago.
Praise God that because of His great love
"we are not consumed, for His compassions never fail."
JONI EARECKSON TADA

Accepting God's love as a gift instead of trying to earn it had
somehow seemed presumptuous and arrogant to me, when,
in fact, my pride was tricking me into thinking that I could
merit His love and forgiveness with my own strength.
LISA WHELCHEL

Being loved by Him whose opinion matters most gives
us the security to risk loving, too—even loving ourselves.
GLORIA GAITHER

There is no pit so deep that God's love is not deeper still.
CORRIE TEN BOOM

More from God's Word

We love him, because he first loved us.
1 JOHN 4:19 KJV

For God so loved the world, that he gave
his only begotten Son, that whosoever believeth in him
should not perish, but have everlasting life.
JOHN 3:16 KJV

For He is gracious and compassionate,
slow to anger, rich in faithful love.
JOEL 2:13 HCSB

Give thanks to Him and praise His name.
For the Lord is good, and His love is eternal;
His faithfulness endures through all generations.
PSALM 100:4–5 HCSB

The LORD's lovingkindnesses indeed never cease,
for His compassions never fail.
They are new every morning. Great is Your faithfulness.
LAMENTATIONS 3:22–23 NASB

A Timely Tip

When all else fails, God's love does not. You can always depend
upon God's love, and He is always your ultimate protection.

48
GOD'S PLAN

*But as it is written: What eye did not see and ear
did not hear, and what never entered the human mind—
God prepared this for those who love Him*
1 CORINTHIANS 2:9 HCSB

God has a plan for this world and for your world. It's a plan that He understands perfectly, a plan that can bring you untold joy now and throughout eternity. But the Lord won't force His plan upon you. He's given you free will, the ability to make choices on your own. The totality of those choices will determine how well you fulfill God's calling.

Sometimes God makes Himself known in obvious ways, but more often His guidance is subtle. So we must be quiet to hear His voice.

If you're a woman who's serious about discovering God's plan for your life—or rediscovering it—start spending quiet time with Him every day. Ask Him for direction. Pray for clarity. And be watchful for His signs. The more time you spend with Him, the sooner the answers will come.

With God, it's never "Plan B" or "second best."
It's always "Plan A." And, if we let Him,
He'll make something beautiful of our lives.
GLORIA GAITHER

God wants us to serve Him with a willing spirit,
one that would choose no other way.
BETH MOORE

The Lord never makes a mistake. One day,
when we are in heaven, I'm sure we shall see the answers
to all the whys. My, how often I have asked, "Why?"
In heaven, we shall see God's side of the embroidery.
CORRIE TEN BOOM

If you believe in a God who controls the big things,
you have to believe in a God who controls the little things.
It is we, of course, to whom things look "little" or "big."
ELISABETH ELLIOT

Ours is an intentional God, brimming over
with motive and mission. He never does things
capriciously or decides with the flip of a coin.
JONI EARECKSON TADA

More from God's Word

"For My thoughts are not your thoughts, and your ways are not My ways." This is the Lord's declaration. "For as heaven is higher than earth, so My ways are higher than your ways, and My thoughts than your thoughts."

Isaiah 55:8–9 HCSB

For whoever does the will of God is My brother and My sister and mother.

Mark 3:35 NKJV

And yet, O Lord, you are our Father. We are the clay, and you are the potter. We all are formed by your hand.

Isaiah 64:8 NLT

It is God who is at work in you, both to will and to work for His good pleasure.

Philippians 2:13 NASB

We must do the works of Him who sent Me while it is day. Night is coming when no one can work.

John 9:4 HCSB

A Timely Tip

God has a wonderful plan for your life. And the time to start looking for that plan—and living it—is now. Discovering God's plan begins with prayer, but it doesn't end there. You've also got to work at it.

49

GOD'S PRESENCE

*For the eyes of the Lord range throughout the earth to show
Himself strong for those whose hearts are completely His.*
2 CHRONICLES 16:9 HCSB

God is everywhere: everywhere you've ever been, everywhere you'll ever be. He is not absent from our world, nor is He absent from your world. God is not "out there"; He is "right here," continuously reshaping His universe, and continuously reshaping the lives of those who dwell in it.

Your Creator is with you always, listening to your thoughts and prayers, watching over your every move. If the demands of everyday life weigh down upon you, you may be tempted to ignore God's presence or—worse yet—to lose faith in His promises. But, when you quiet yourself and acknowledge His presence, God will touch your heart and renew your strength.

Psalm 46:10 remind us to "Be still, and know that I am God."NIV. When we do, we can be comforted in the knowledge that God does not love us from a distance. He is not just near. He is here.

It is God to whom and with whom we travel;
while He is the End of our journey,
He is also at every stopping place.
ELISABETH ELLIOT

Through the death and broken body
of Jesus Christ on the Cross,
you and I have been given access
to the presence of God when we approach
Him by faith in prayer.
ANNE GRAHAM LOTZ

Do not limit the limitless God!
With Him, face the future unafraid
because you are never alone.
LETTIE COWMAN

Worship is an inward reverence, the bowing down
of the soul in the presence of God.
ELIZABETH GEORGE

The love of God is so vast,
the power of His touch so invigorating,
we could just stay in His presence for hours,
soaking up His glory, basking in His blessings.
DEBRA EVANS

More from God's Word

*You will seek Me and find Me when you
search for Me with all your heart.*
JEREMIAH 29:13 HCSB

*I know the LORD is always with me.
I will not be shaken, for he is right beside me.*
PSALM 16:8 NLT

Draw near to God, and He will draw near to you.
JAMES 4:8 HCSB

*Though I walk through the valley of the shadow of death,
I will fear no evil: for thou art with me.*
PSALM 23:4 KJV

I am not alone, because the Father is with Me.
JOHN 16:32 NKJV

A Timely Tip

God isn't far away—He's right here, right now. And He's
willing to talk to you right here, right now.

50

God's Promises

Let us hold on to the confession of our hope
without wavering, for He who promised is faithful.
HEBREWS 10:23 HCSB

The Bible contains promises upon which you, as a believer, can depend. When the Creator of the universe makes a pledge to you, He will keep it. No exceptions.

You can think of the Bible as a written contract between you and your heavenly Father. When you fulfill your obligations to Him, the Lord will most certainly fulfill His covenant to you.

When we accept Christ into our hearts, God promises us the opportunity to experience contentment, peace, and spiritual abundance. But more importantly, God promises that the priceless gift of eternal life will be ours. These promises should give us comfort. With God on our side, we have absolutely nothing to fear in this world and everything to hope for in the next.

Claim all of God's promises in the Bible. Your sins, your worries, your life—you may cast them all on Him.

CORRIE TEN BOOM

Brother, is your faith looking upward today?
Trust in the promise of the Savior.
Sister, is the light shining bright on your way?
Trust in the promise of thy Lord.

FANNY CROSBY

Faith isn't the ability to believe long and far
into the misty future. It's simply taking
God at His word and taking the next step.

JONI EARECKSON TADA

Gather the riches of God's promises which can
strengthen you in the time when there will be no freedom.

CORRIE TEN BOOM

The meaning of hope isn't just some flimsy wishing.
It's a firm confidence in God's promises—
that He will ultimately set things right.

SHEILA WALSH

More from God's Word

Sustain me as You promised, and I will live;
do not let me be ashamed of my hope.
PSALM 119:116 HCSB

They will bind themselves to the LORD with an eternal
covenant that will never again be broken.
JEREMIAH 50:5 NLT

As for God, his way is perfect: the word of the LORD is tried:
he is a buckler to all those that trust in him.
PSALM 18:30 KJV

My God is my rock, in whom I take refuge,
my shield and the horn of my salvation.
2 SAMUEL 22:2–3 NIV

He heeded their prayer, because they put their trust in him.
1 CHRONICLES 5:20 NKJV

A Timely Tip

God has made many promises to you, and He will keep every single one of them. Your job is to trust God's Word and to live accordingly.

51

GOD'S PROTECTION

The LORD is my shepherd, I shall not want.
He makes me lie down in green pastures;
He leads me beside quiet waters. He restores my soul.

PSALM 23:1–3 NASB

God's love encircles us and comforts us in times of adversity. In times of hardship, He restores our strength; in times of sorrow, He dries our tears. When we are troubled, or weak, or embittered, God is as near as our next breath.

God has promised to protect us, and He intends to fulfill His promise. In a world filled with dangers and temptations, God is the ultimate armor. In a world filled with misleading messages, God's Word is the ultimate truth. In a world filled with more frustrations than we can count, God's Son offers the ultimate peace.

Will you accept God's peace and wear God's armor against the dangers of our world? Hopefully so, because when you do, you can live courageously, knowing that you possess the ultimate protection: God's unfailing love for you.

Prayer is our pathway not only to divine protection,
but also to a personal, intimate relationship with God.
SHIRLEY DOBSON

The Lord God of heaven and earth, the Almighty Creator
of all things, He who holds the universe in His hand as though
it were a very little thing, He is your Shepherd, and He has
charged Himself with the care and keeping of you, as a shepherd
is charged with the care and keeping of his sheep.
HANNAH WHITALL SMITH

He goes before us, follows behind us,
and hems us safe inside the realm of His protection.
BETH MOORE

He is within and without. His Spirit dwells within me.
His armor protects me. He goes before me and is behind me.
MARY MORRISON SUGGS

In all the old castles of England, there was a place called
the keep. It was always the strongest and best protected place
in the castle, and in it were hidden all who were weak and
helpless and unable to defend themselves in times of danger.
Shall we be afraid to hide ourselves in the keeping power
of our Divine Keeper, who neither slumbers nor sleeps,
and who has promised to preserve our going out and our
coming in, from this time forth and even forever more?
HANNAH WHITALL SMITH

MORE FROM GOD'S WORD

The LORD is my light and my salvation—
whom should I fear? The LORD is the stronghold of my life—
of whom should I be afraid?
PSALM 27:1 HCSB

The LORD is my rock, my fortress, and my deliverer, my God,
my mountain where I seek refuge. My shield, the horn of my
salvation, my stronghold, my refuge, and my Savior.
2 SAMUEL 22:2–3 HCSB

As for God, His way is perfect; the word of the LORD
is proven; He is a shield to all who trust in Him.
PSALM 18:30 NKJV

Those who trust in the LORD are like Mount Zion.
It cannot be shaken; it remains forever.
PSALM 125:1 HCSB

So we may boldly say: "The Lord is my helper;
I will not fear. What can man do to me?"
HEBREWS 13:6 NKJV

A TIMELY TIP

Earthly security is an illusion. Your only real security comes from the loving heart of God. If you seek maximum protection, there's only one place you can receive it: from an infinite God.

52

GOD'S SUFFICIENCY

My grace is sufficient for you,
for my power is made perfect in weakness.
2 CORINTHIANS 12:9 NIV

Of this you can be sure: the loving heart of God is sufficient to meet your needs. Whatever dangers you may face, whatever heartbreaks you must endure, God is with you, and He stands ready to comfort you and to heal you.

The psalmist writes, "Weeping may endure for a night, but joy comes in the morning" (Psalm 30:5 NKJV). But when we are suffering, the morning may seem very far away. It is not. God promises that He is "near to those who have a broken heart" (Psalm 34:18 NKJV). In times of intense sadness, we must turn to Him, and we must encourage our friends and family members to do likewise.

If you are experiencing the intense pain of a recent loss, or if you are still mourning a loss from long ago, perhaps you are now ready to begin the next stage of your journey with God. If so, be mindful of this fact: the loving heart of God is sufficient to meet any challenge, including yours. Trust the sufficient heart of God.

Yes, God's grace is always sufficient,
and His arms are always open to give it.
But, will our arms be open to receive it?
BETH MOORE

God's all-sufficiency is a major.
Your inability is a minor.
Major in majors, not in minors.
CORRIE TEN BOOM

The last and greatest lesson that the soul has to learn
is the fact that God, and God alone, is enough
for all its needs. This is the lesson that all His dealings
with us are meant to teach; and this is the crowning
discovery of our whole Christian life. God is enough!
HANNAH WHITALL SMITH

Of course you will encounter trouble.
But behold a God of power who can take
any evil and turn it into a door of hope.
CATHERINE MARSHALL

God is, must be, our answer to every question
and every cry of need.
HANNAH WHITALL SMITH

More from God's Word

*And my God will supply all your needs according
to His riches in glory in Christ Jesus.*
PHILIPPIANS 4:19 HCSB

*And God is able to make every grace overflow to you,
so that in every way, always having everything you need,
you may excel in every good work.*
2 CORINTHIANS 9:8 HCSB

*For the eyes of the Lord are on the righteous,
and His ears are open to their prayers;
but the face of the Lord is against those who do evil.*
1 PETER 3:12 NKJV

*The LORD is my strength and song, and He has become
my salvation; He is my God, and I will praise Him.*
EXODUS 15:2 NKJV

*Take My yoke upon you and learn from Me, because I am
gentle and humble in heart, and you will find rest for your
souls. For My yoke is easy and My burden is light.*
MATTHEW 11:29–30 HCSB

A Timely Tip

God is sufficient. Whatever you really need, He can provide.
Whatever your weakness, He is stronger. And His strength will help
you measure up to the tasks He intends for you to accomplish.

53

GOD'S SUPPORT

Nevertheless God, who comforts
the downcast, comforted us.
2 CORINTHIANS 7:6 NKJV

God's Word promises that He will support you in good times and comfort you in hard times. The Creator of the universe stands ready to give you the strength to meet any challenge and the courage to face any adversity. When you ask for God's help, He responds in His own way and at His own appointed hour. But make no mistake: He always responds.

In a world brimming with dangers and temptations, God is the ultimate armor. In a world saturated with misleading messages, God's Word is the ultimate truth. In a world filled with frustrations and distractions, God's Son offers the ultimate peace.

Today, as you encounter the inevitable challenges of everyday life, remember that your heavenly Father never leaves you, not even for a moment. He's always available, always ready to listen, always ready to lead. When you make a habit of talking to Him early and often, He'll guide you and comfort you every day of your life.

No matter what we are going through,
no matter how long the waiting for answers,
of one thing we may be sure. God is faithful.
He keeps His promises. What he starts,
He finishes, including His perfect work in us.
GLORIA GAITHER

Put your hand into the hand of God.
He gives the calmness and serenity of heart and soul.
LETTIE COWMAN

When the dream of our heart is one
that God has planted there, a strange happiness
flows into us. At that moment, the spiritual resources
of the universe are released to help us.
CATHERINE MARSHALL

The Lord God of heaven and earth, the Almighty Creator,
He who holds the universe in His hand as though
it were a very little thing, He is your Shepherd,
and He has charged Himself with the care and keeping of you.
HANNAH WHITALL SMITH

Measure the size of the obstacles against the size of God.
BETH MOORE

More from God's Word

My grace is sufficient for you,
for my power is made perfect in weakness.
2 Corinthians 12:9 NIV

Therefore humble yourselves under
the mighty hand of God, that He may exalt you in due time,
casting all your care upon Him, for He cares for you.
1 Peter 5:6–7 NKJV

Therefore, we may boldly say: The Lord is my helper;
I will not be afraid. What can man do to me?
Hebrews 13:6 HCSB

The Lord is my light and my salvation—
whom should I fear? The Lord is the stronghold of my life—
of whom should I be afraid?
Psalm 27:1 HCSB

The Lord is my shepherd; I shall not want.
He makes me to lie down in green pastures;
He leads me beside the still waters. He restores my soul.
Psalm 23:1–3 NKJV

A Timely Tip

Whatever your weaknesses, God is stronger. And His strength will help you measure up to His tasks.

54

GOD'S TIMING

Therefore humble yourselves under the mighty hand of God,
that He may exalt you in due time.

1 PETER 5:6 NKJV

If you're like most people, you're in a hurry. You know precisely what you want, and you know precisely when you want it: as soon as possible. Because your time on earth is limited, you may feel a sense of urgency. God does not. There is no panic in heaven.

Our heavenly Father, in His infinite wisdom, operates according to His own timetable, not ours. He has plans that we cannot see and purposes that we cannot know. He has created a world that unfolds according to His own schedule. Thank goodness! After all, He is omniscient; He is trustworthy; and He knows what's best for us.

If you've been waiting impatiently for the Lord to answer your prayers, it's time to put a stop to all that needless worry. You can be sure that God will answer your prayers when the time is right. Your job is to keep praying—and working—until He does.

When our plans are interrupted, His are not.
His plans are proceeding exactly as scheduled,
moving us always—including those minutes or hours
or years which seem most useless or wasted or unendurable—
toward the goal of true maturity.
ELISABETH ELLIOT

Your times are in His hands.
He's in charge of the timetable, so wait patiently.
KAY ARTHUR

God's delays and His ways can be confusing
because the process God uses to accomplish His will
can go against human logic and common sense.
ANNE GRAHAM LOTZ

When we read of the great Biblical leaders,
we see that it was not uncommon for God
to ask them to wait, not just a day or two,
but for years, until God was ready for them to act.
GLORIA GAITHER

He wants us to have a faith that does not complain
while waiting, but rejoices because we know our times are in
His hands—nail-scarred hands that labor for our highest good.
KAY ARTHUR

More from God's Word

He has made everything appropriate in its time.
He has also put eternity in their hearts, but man cannot
discover the work God has done from beginning to end.
ECCLESIASTES 3:11 HCSB

Yet the LORD longs to be gracious to you;
he rises to show you compassion. For the LORD
is a God of justice. Blessed are all who wait for him!
ISAIAH 30:18 NIV

Those who trust in the LORD are like Mount Zion.
It cannot be shaken; it remains forever.
PSALM 125:1 HCSB

Trust in the LORD with all your heart,
and lean not on your own understanding; in all your ways
acknowledge Him, and He shall direct your paths.
PROVERBS 3:5–6 NKJV

To every thing there is a season,
and a time to every purpose under the heaven.
ECCLESIASTES 3:1 KJV

A Timely Tip

Although you don't know precisely what you need—or when
you need it—God does. So trust His timing.

55

GOD'S WILL

Teach me to do Your will, for You are my God;
Your Spirit is good. Lead me in the land of uprightness.
PSALM 143:10 NKJV

As human beings with limited understanding, we can never fully comprehend the will of God. But as believers in a benevolent God, we must always *trust* the will of our heavenly Father.

Before His crucifixion, Jesus went to the Mount of Olives and poured out His heart to God (Luke 22). Jesus knew of the agony that He was destined to endure, but He also knew that God's will must be done. We, like our Savior, face trials that bring fear and trembling to the very depths of our souls, but like Christ, we, too, must ultimately seek God's will, not our own.

As this day unfolds, seek God's will for your own life and obey His Word. When you entrust your life to Him completely and without reservation, He will give you the strength to meet any challenge, the courage to face any trial, and the wisdom to live in His righteousness and in His peace.

In the center of a hurricane there is absolute quiet and peace.
There is no safer place than in the center of the will of God.
CORRIE TEN BOOM

The only safe place is in the center of God's will.
It is not only the safest place. It is also the most
rewarding and the most satisfying place to be.
GIGI GRAHAM TCHIVIDJIAN

The center of power is not to be found in summit meetings
or in peace conferences. It is not in Peking or Washington
or the United Nations, but rather where a child of God prays
in the power of the Spirit for God's will to be done in her life,
in her home, and in the world around her.
RUTH BELL GRAHAM

In the Garden of Gethsemane,
Jesus went through agony of soul in His efforts
to resist the temptation to do what
He felt like doing rather than what
He knew was God's will for Him.
JOYCE MEYER

The will of God is the most delicious
and delightful thing in the universe.
HANNAH WHITALL SMITH

More from God's Word

Commit to the LORD whatever you do,
and he will establish your plans.
PROVERBS 16:3 NIV

Then Jesus explained: "My nourishment
comes from doing the will of God, who sent me,
and from finishing his work."
JOHN 4:34 NLT

For it is God who is working in you, enabling you
both to desire and to work out His good purpose.
PHILIPPIANS 2:13 HCSB

For it is better, if it is the will of God,
to suffer for doing good than for doing evil.
1 PETER 3:17 NKJV

He is the LORD. He will do what He thinks is good.
1 SAMUEL 3:18 HCSB

A Timely Tip

Even when you cannot understand God's plans, you must trust them. If you place yourself in the center of God's will, He will provide for your needs and direct your path.

56

GOD'S WORD

*For the word of God is living and effective
and sharper than any two-edged sword,
penetrating as far as to divide soul, spirit,
joints, and marrow; it is a judge of the ideas
and thoughts of the heart.*

HEBREWS 4:12 HCSB

God's Word is unlike any other book. The Bible is a roadmap for life here on earth and for life eternal. As Christians, we are called upon to study God's holy Word, to trust its promises, to follow its commandments, and to share its Good News with the world.

As believers, we must study the Bible and meditate upon its meaning for our lives. Otherwise, we deprive ourselves of a priceless gift from our Creator. God's Holy Word is, indeed, a transforming, life-changing, one-of-a-kind treasure. And, a passing acquaintance with the Good Book is insufficient for Christians who seek to obey God's Word and to understand His will. After all, neither man nor woman should live by bread alone.

I need the spiritual revival that comes from
spending quiet time alone with Jesus in prayer
and in thoughtful meditation on His Word.
ANNE GRAHAM LOTZ

Only through routine, regular exposure
to God's Word can you and I draw out
the nutrition needed to grow a heart of faith.
ELIZABETH GEORGE

The Bible became a living book and a guide for my life.
VONETTE BRIGHT

Weave the unveiling fabric of God's Word
through your heart and mind.
It will hold strong, even if the rest of life unravels.
GIGI GRAHAM TCHIVIDJIAN

Words fail to express my love for this holy Book,
my gratitude for its author, for His love and goodness.
How shall I thank Him for it?
LOTTIE MOON

More from God's Word

Jesus answered, "It is written: 'Man does not live by bread alone, but on every word that comes from the mouth of God.'"
MATTHEW 4:4 NIV

Therefore everyone who hears these words of mine and puts them into practice is like a wise man who built his house on the rock.
MATTHEW 7:24-25 NIV

All Scripture is given by inspiration of God, and is profitable for doctrine, for reproof, for correction, for instruction in righteousness.
2 TIMOTHY 3:16 KJV

Your word is a lamp for my feet and a light on my path.
PSALM 119:105 HCSB

A Timely Tip

God intends for you to use His Word as your guidebook for life. Your intentions should be the same.

57

HAPPINESS

Those who listen to instruction will prosper;
those who trust the LORD will be joyful.
PROVERBS 16:20 NLT

Everywhere we turn, or so it seems, the message is clear: happiness is for sale, and if we have enough money, we can buy it. But God's Word contains a different message. In the Bible, we are taught that happiness is a byproduct, the result of living in harmony with God's plan for our lives. Obedience is the path to peace, love, and happiness. Disobedience is the path to discouragement, dissatisfaction, and doubt.

Happiness also depends on the way we think. If we form the habit of focusing on the positive aspects of life, we tend to be happier. But, if we choose to dwell on the negatives, our very own thoughts have the power to make us miserable.

Do you want to be a happy Christian? Then you must start by being an obedient Christian. Then, you must set your mind and heart upon God's blessings. When you think about it, you have many reasons to be joyful. When you count your blessings every day—and obey your Creator—you'll discover that happiness is not a commodity to be purchased; it is, instead, the natural consequence of walking daily with God.

We will never be happy until we
make God the source of our fulfillment.
STORMIE OMARTIAN

When we bring sunshine into the lives of others,
we're warmed by it ourselves.
When we spill a little happiness, it splashes on us.
BARBARA JOHNSON

When we do what is right, we have contentment,
peace, and happiness.
BEVERLY LAHAYE

The truth is that even in the midst of trouble,
happy moments swim by us every day,
like shining fish waiting to be caught.
BARBARA JOHNSON

How happy we are when we realize
that He is responsible, that He goes before,
that goodness and mercy shall follow us!
LETTIE COWMAN

More from God's Word

If they obey and serve him, they will spend the rest of their days in prosperity and their years in contentment.
JOB 36:11 NIV

Happiness makes a person smile, but sadness can break a person's spirit.
PROVERBS 15:13 NCV

I have come that they may have life, and that they may have it more abundantly.
JOHN 10:10 NKJV

A joyful heart is good medicine, but a broken spirit dries up the bones.
PROVERBS 17:22 HCSB

Joyful is the person who finds wisdom, the one who gains understanding.
PROVERBS 3:13 NLT

A Timely Tip

The best day to be happy is this one. Don't spend your whole life in the waiting room. Make up your mind to celebrate today.

58

HELPING OTHERS

*Carry one another's burdens;
in this way you will fulfill the law of Christ.*
GALATIANS 6:2 HCSB

If you're looking for somebody to help, you won't have to look very far. Somebody very nearby needs a helping hand, or a hot meal, or a pat on the back, or a prayer. In order to find that person, you'll need to keep your eyes and your heart open, and you'll need to stay focused on the needs of others. Focusing, however, is not as simple as it seems.

We live in a fast-paced, media-driven world filled with countless temptations and time-wasting distractions. Sometimes we may convince ourselves that we simply don't have the time or the resources to offer help to the needy. Such thoughts are misguided. Caring for our neighbors must be our priority because it is God's priority.

God has a specific plan for your life, and part of that plan involves service to His children. Service is not a burden; it's an opportunity. Seize your opportunity today. Tomorrow may be too late.

*The measure of a life, after all,
is not its duration but its donation.*
CORRIE TEN BOOM

*It is one of the most beautiful compensations
of life that no one can sincerely
try to help another without helping herself.*
BARBARA JOHNSON

*What is needed for happy effectual service
is simply to put your work into the Lord's hand,
and leave it there.*
HANNAH WHITALL SMITH

*Life is not salvage to be saved out of the world,
but an investment to be used in the world.*
LETTIE COWMAN

*Doing something positive toward another person
is a practical approach to feeling good about yourself.*
BARBARA JOHNSON

More from God's Word

*Let us not become weary in doing good, for at the proper time
we will reap a harvest if we do not give up.*
GALATIANS 6:9 NIV

*If you have two shirts, give one to the poor.
If you have food, share it with those who are hungry.*
LUKE 3:11 NLT

Whenever you are able, do good to people who need help.
PROVERBS 3:27 NCV

*Whatever you did for one of the least of these
brothers of Mine, you did for Me.*
MATTHEW 25:40 HCSB

*Therefore, as we have opportunity, we must work for the good
of all, especially for those who belong to the household of faith.*
GALATIANS 6:10 HCSB

A Timely Tip

The direction of your steps and the quality of your life will be
determined by the level of your service. Someone very nearby needs
your help today. And the next move is yours.

59

HOPE

Let us hold fast the confession of our hope without wavering,
for He who promised is faithful.

HEBREWS 10:23 NASB

God's promises give up hope: hope for today, hope for tomorrow, hope for all eternity. The hope that the world offers is temporary, at best. But the hope that God offers never grows old and never goes out of date. It's no wonder, then, that when we pin our hopes on worldly resources, we are often disappointed. Thankfully, God has no such record of failure.

The Bible teaches that the Lord blesses those who trust in His wisdom and follow in the footsteps of His Son. Will you count yourself among that number? When you do, you'll have every reason on earth—and in heaven—to be hopeful about your future. After all, God has made important promises to you, promises that He is certainly going to keep. So be hopeful, be optimistic, be faithful, and do your best. Then, leave the rest up to God. Your destiny is safe with Him.

Never yield to gloomy anticipation.
Place your hope and confidence in God.
He has no record of failure.
LETTIE COWMAN

Hope is the desire and the ability to move forward.
EMILIE BARNES

Love is the seed of all hope.
It is the enticement to trust, to risk,
to try, and to go on.
GLORIA GAITHER

Of course you will encounter trouble.
But behold a God of power who can take any evil
and turn it into a door of hope.
CATHERINE MARSHALL

No other religion, no other philosophy
promises new bodies, hearts, and minds.
Only in the gospel of Christ
do hurting people find such incredible hope.
JONI EARECKSON TADA

More from God's Word

*This hope we have as an anchor of the soul,
a hope both sure and steadfast.*
HEBREWS 6:19 NASB

*The LORD is good to those who wait for Him,
to the soul who seeks Him. It is good that one should hope
and wait quietly for the salvation of the LORD.*
LAMENTATIONS 3:25–26 NKJV

I say to myself, "The LORD is mine, so I hope in him."
LAMENTATIONS 3:24 NCV

Hope deferred makes the heart sick.
PROVERBS 13:12 NKJV

*Be strong and courageous,
all you who put your hope in the LORD.*
PSALM 31:24 HCSB

A Timely Tip

Since God has promised to guide and protect you—now and forever—you should never lose hope.

60
JESUS

The next day John saw Jesus coming toward him
and said, "Here is the Lamb of God,
who takes away the sin of the world!"
JOHN 1:29 HCSB

Our circumstances change, but Jesus does not. Even when the world seems to be trembling between our feet, Jesus remains the spiritual bedrock that cannot be moved. God speaks to us through the love and sacrifice of His Son. If we're wise, we will listen to Jesus, we will learn from Him, and we will follow Him.

He was the Son of God, but He wore a crown of thorns. He was the Savior of mankind, yet He was put to death on a roughhewn cross. He offered His healing touch to an unsaved world, and yet the same hands that had healed the sick and raised the dead were pierced with nails. Christ showed enduring love for His believers by willingly sacrificing His own life so that we might have eternal life. Let us love Him, praise Him, and share His message of salvation with our neighbors and with the world.

*Christ, the Son of God, the complete embodiment
of God's Word, came among us. He looked
on humanity's losing battle with sin and pitched
His divine tent in the middle of the camp
so that He could dwell among us.*

BETH MOORE

*Once we recognize our need for Jesus,
then the building of our faith begins.
It is a daily, moment-by-moment life
of absolute dependence upon Him for everything.*

CATHERINE MARSHALL

Jesus is all compassion. He never betrays us.

CATHERINE MARSHALL

*When you are weary and everything
seems to be going wrong, you can still
utter these four words: "I trust You, Jesus."*

SARAH YOUNG

*Jesus is Victor. Calvary is the place of victory.
Obedience is the pathway of victory. Bible study
and prayer is the preparation for victory.*

CORRIE TEN BOOM

More from God's Word

Jesus Christ the same yesterday, and today, and for ever.
HEBREWS 13:8 KJV

I have come as a light into the world, that whoever believes in Me should not abide in darkness.
JOHN 12:46 NKJV

I am the good shepherd. The good shepherd gives His life for the sheep.
JOHN 10:11 NKJV

Who can separate us from the love of Christ? Can affliction or anguish or persecution or famine or nakedness or danger or sword? . . . No, in all these things we are more than victorious through Him who loved us.
ROMANS 8:35, 37 HCSB

The thief's purpose is to steal and kill and destroy. My purpose is to them a rich and satisfying life.
JOHN 10:10 NLT

A Timely Tip

Jesus loves you, and He offers you eternal life with Him in heaven. Welcome Him into your heart now! And once you've done so, begin to use His teachings to help you prioritize every aspect of your life.

61
JOY

This is the day which the LORD has made;
let us rejoice and be glad in it.
PSALM 118:24 NASB

The joy that the world offers is fleeting and incomplete: here today, gone tomorrow, not coming back anytime soon. But God's joy is different. His joy has staying power. In fact, it's a gift that never stops giving to those who welcome His Son.

Psalm 100 reminds us to celebrate the lives that God has given us: "Shout for joy to the LORD, all the earth. Worship the LORD with gladness; come before Him with joyful songs." (v. 1–2 NIV). Yet sometimes, amid the inevitable complications and predicaments that are woven into the fabric of everyday life, we forget to rejoice. Instead of celebrating life, we complain about it. This is an understandable mistake, but a mistake nonetheless. As Christians, we are called by our Creator to live joyfully and abundantly. To do otherwise is to squander His spiritual gifts.

This day and every day, Christ offers you His peace and His joy. Accept it and share it with others, just as He has shared His joy with you.

Finding joy means first of all finding Jesus.
JILL BRISCOE

*The Christian lifestyle is not one of legalistic do's and don'ts,
but one that is positive, attractive, and joyful.*
VONETTE BRIGHT

*Joy is the heart vibrating in grateful rhythm
to the love of Almighty God who actually chooses
to make His home within us.*
SUSAN LENZKES

*It is the definition of joy to be able to offer back
to God the essence of what He's placed in you,
be that creativity or a love of ideas
or a compassionate heart or the gift of hospitality.*
PAULA RINEHART

*A joyful heart is the inevitable result
of a heart burning with love.*
MOTHER TERESA

More from God's Word

Rejoice in the Lord always. Again I will say, rejoice!
PHILIPPIANS 4:4 NKJV

*I have spoken these things to you so that My joy
may be in you and your joy may be complete.*
JOHN 15:11 HCSB

*Rejoice always, pray without ceasing, in everything give thanks;
for this is the will of God in Christ Jesus for you.*
1 THESSALONIANS 5:16-18 NKJV

*Until now you have asked for nothing in My name.
Ask and you will receive, that your joy may be complete.*
JOHN 16:24 HCSB

*So you also have sorrow now. But I will see you again.
Your hearts will rejoice, and no one will rob you of your joy.*
JOHN 16:22 HCSB

A Timely Tip

Every day, God gives you many reasons to rejoice. The gifts are
His, but the rejoicing is up to you.

62

JUDGING OTHERS

Judge not, and you shall not be judged. Condemn not, and you shall not be condemned. Forgive, and you will be forgiven.

LUKE 6:37 NKJV

The need to judge others seems woven into the very fabric of human consciousness. We mortals feel compelled to serve as informal judges and juries, pronouncing our own verdicts on the actions and perceived motivations of others, all the while excusing—or oftentimes hiding—our own shortcomings. But God's Word instructs us to let Him be the judge. He knows that we, with our limited knowledge and personal biases, are simply ill-equipped to assess the actions of others. The act of judging, then, becomes not only an act of futility, but also an affront to our Creator.

When Jesus came upon a woman who had been condemned by the Pharisees, He spoke not only to the people who had gathered there, but also to all generations. Christ warned, "He that is without sin among you, let him first cast a stone at her" (John 8:7 KJV). The message is clear: because we are all sinners, we must refrain from the temptation to judging others.

So the next time you're tempted to cast judgment on another human being, resist that temptation. God hasn't called you to be a judge; He's called you to be a witness.

Judging draws the judgment of others.
CATHERINE MARSHALL

Perhaps the greatest blessing that
religious inheritance can bestow is an open mind,
one that can listen without judging.
KATHLEEN NORRIS

Only Christ can free us from the prison of legalism,
and then only if we are willing to be freed.
MADELEINE L'ENGLE

Don't judge other people more harshly
than you want God to judge you.
MARIE T. FREEMAN

It's hard to criticize someone
if you are praying for them.
ELIZABETH GEORGE

More from God's Word

Don't criticize one another, brothers.
He who criticizes a brother or judges his brother
criticizes the law and judges the law. But if you
judge the law, you are not a doer of the law but a judge.
James 4:11 HCSB

Do everything without grumbling and arguing,
so that you may be blameless and pure.
Philippians 2:14–15 HCSB

Therefore, anyone of you who judges is without excuse.
For when you judge another, you condemn yourself,
since you, the judge, do the same things.
Romans 2:1 HCSB

Those who guard their lips preserve their lives,
but those who speak rashly will come to ruin.
Proverbs 13:3 NIV

Let the words of my mouth and the meditation
of my heart be acceptable in Your sight,
O Lord, my strength and my Redeemer.
Psalm 19:14 NKJV

A Timely Tip

To the extent you judge others, so, too, will you be judged. So you must, to the best of your ability, refrain from judgmental thoughts and words.

63

KINDNESS

Therefore, whatever you want men to do to you,
do also to them, for this is the Law and the Prophets.
MATTHEW 7:12 NKJV

Kindness is a choice. Sometimes, when we feel happy or prosperous, we find it easy to be kind. Other times, when we are discouraged or tired, we can scarcely summon the energy to utter a single kind word. But, God's commandment is clear: we must observe the Golden Rule "in everything." God intends that we make the conscious choice to treat others with kindness and respect, no matter our circumstances, no matter our emotions. Kindness, therefore, is a choice that we, as Christians, must make many times each day.

When we weave the thread of kindness into the very fabric of our lives, we give a priceless gift to others, and we give glory to the One who gave His life for us. As believers, we must do no less.

The goodness you receive from God
is a treasure for you to share with others.
ELIZABETH GEORGE

Sometimes one little spark of kindness
is all it takes to reignite the light of hope
in a heart that's blinded by pain.
BARBARA JOHNSON

It is one of the most beautiful compensations
of life that no one can sincerely try
to help another without helping herself.
BARBARA JOHNSON

Kindness in this world will do much to help others,
not only to come into the light,
but also to grow in grace day by day.
FANNY CROSBY

Showing kindness to others is one
of the nicest things we can do for ourselves.
JANETTE OKE

More from God's Word

A new commandment I give unto you, that ye love one another;
as I have loved you, that ye also love one another.
JOHN 13:34 KJV

Be kind to one another, tender-hearted, forgiving each other,
just as God in Christ also has forgiven you.
EPHESIANS 4:32 NASB

Who is wise and has understanding among you? He should
show his works by good conduct with wisdom's gentleness.
JAMES 3:13 HCSB

And let us not grow weary while doing good,
for in due season we shall reap if we do not lose heart.
GALATIANS 6:9 NKJV

Assuredly, I say to you, inasmuch as you did it to one
of the least of these My brethren, you did it to Me.
MATTHEW 25:40 NKJV

A Timely Tip

Kind words and good deeds have echoes that last a lifetime and beyond. Kind words cost nothing, but when they're spoken at the right time, they can be priceless.

64
LIFE

*I urge you to live a life worthy
of the calling you have received.*
EPHESIANS 4:1 NIV

Life is a glorious gift from God. Treat it that way.

This day, like every other, is filled to the brim with opportunities, challenges, and choices. But no choice that you make is more important than the choice you make concerning God. Today, you will either place Him at the center of your life—or not—and the consequences of that choice have implications that are both temporal and eternal.

Sometimes we don't intentionally neglect God; we simply allow ourselves to become overwhelmed with the demands of everyday life. And then, without our even realizing it, we gradually drift away from the One we need most. Thankfully, God never drifts away from us. He remains always present, always steadfast, always loving.

As you begin this day, place God and His Son where they belong: in your head, in your prayers, on your lips, and in your heart. And then, with God as your guide and companion, let the journey begin . . .

The measure of a life, after all,
is not its duration but its donation.
CORRIE TEN BOOM

Life becomes inspiring, not in spite of the problems
and hard hits, but because of them.
JONI EARECKSON TADA

Life is not salvage to be saved out of the world,
but an investment to be used in the world.
LETTIE COWMAN

When God is in sharp focus,
then life is also undistorted.
ELIZABETH GEORGE

Life is immortal, love eternal;
death is nothing but a horizon,
and a horizon is only the limit of our vision.
CORRIE TEN BOOM

MORE FROM GOD'S WORD

*Jesus said to her, "I am the resurrection and the life.
The one who believes in Me, even if he dies, will live.
Everyone who lives and believes in Me
will never die—ever. Do you believe this?"*
JOHN 11:25–26 HCSB

*He who follows righteousness and mercy finds life,
righteousness, and honor.*
PROVERBS 21:21 NKJV

*And Jesus said unto them, I am the bread of life:
he that cometh to me shall never hunger;
and he that believeth on me shall never thirst.*
JOHN 6:35 KJV

*Whoever finds their life will lose it,
and whoever loses their life for my sake will find it.*
MATTHEW 10:39 NIV

*You will teach me how to live a holy life. Being with you will
fill me with joy; at your right hand I will find pleasure forever.*
PSALM 16:11 NCV

A TIMELY TIP

Your life is a priceless opportunity, a gift of incalculable worth. Be thankful to the Giver and use His gift wisely while there's still time because night is coming when no one can work.

65

LIGHT

This is the message which we have heard from Him and declare to you, that God is light and in Him is no darkness at all.
1 JOHN 1:5 NKJV

Matthew 5 makes it clear: you are, indeed, "the light" of this world (v. 14). Corrie ten Boom observed, "There is nothing anybody else can do that can stop God from using us. We can turn everything into a testimony." Her words remind us that when we decide to speak up for God, our actions may speak even more loudly than our words.

When we demonstrate our faith through service, we are fulfilling an important responsibility: the responsibility of making certain that our words are reinforced by our actions. When we share our testimonies through both words *and* service, we become undeniable examples of the changes that Jesus makes in the lives of those who accept Him as their Savior.

Are you willing to follow in the footsteps of Jesus by dedicating yourself to a life of service? If so, you should also be willing to talk about Him. And make no mistake—the time to express your belief in Him is now. You know how He has touched your own heart; help Him do the same for others.

His life is our light—our purpose
and meaning and reason for living.
ANNE GRAHAM LOTZ

You have to look for the joy.
Look for the light of God that is hitting your life,
and you will find sparkles you didn't know were there.
BARBARA JOHNSON

Walk in the daylight of God's will
because then you will be safe; you will not stumble.
ANNE GRAHAM LOTZ

Light is stronger than darkness—
darkness cannot "comprehend" or "overcome" it.
ANNE GRAHAM LOTZ

God's guidance is even more important
than common sense. I can declare that the deepest darkness
is outshone by the light of Jesus.
CORRIE TEN BOOM

More from God's Word

I have come as a light into the world, so that everyone
who believes in Me would not remain in darkness.
JOHN 12:46 HCSB

LORD, You are my lamp; the LORD illuminates my darkness.
2 SAMUEL 22:29 HCSB

For you were once darkness, but now you are light in the Lord.
Walk as children of light—for the fruit of the light
results in all goodness, righteousness, and truth—
discerning what is pleasing to the Lord.
EPHESIANS 5:8–10 HCSB

He who loves his brother abides in the light,
and there is no cause for stumbling in him.
1 JOHN 2:10 NKJV

You are the light that gives light to the world. . . . In the same
way, you should be a light for other people. Live so that they
will see the good things you do and will praise your Father in
heaven.
MATTHEW 5:14, 16 NCV

A Timely Tip

Jesus is the light of the world. Make sure that you are capturing
and reflecting His light.

66
LISTENING TO GOD

Be still, and know that I am God.
PSALM 46:10 KJV

God speaks to us in different ways at different times. Sometimes He speaks loudly and clearly. But more often He speaks in a quiet voice, and if you are wise, you will be listening carefully when He does. To do so, you must carve out quiet moments each day to study His Word and to sense His direction.

Are you willing to pray sincerely and then to wait quietly for God's response? Can you quiet yourself long enough to listen to your conscience? Are you attuned to the subtle guidance of your intuition? Hopefully so. Usually God refrains from sending His messages on stone tablets or city billboards. More often, He communicates in subtler ways. If you sincerely desire to hear His voice, you must listen carefully, and you must do so in the silent corners of your quiet, willing heart.

Deep within the center of the soul is a chamber of peace
where God lives and where, if we will enter it and quiet
all the other sounds, we can hear His gentle whisper.
LETTIE COWMAN

When we come to Jesus stripped of pretensions,
with a needy spirit, ready to listen,
He meets us at the point of need.
CATHERINE MARSHALL

The purpose of all prayer is to find God's will
and to make that our prayer.
CATHERINE MARSHALL

I am Thine, O Lord;
I have heard Thy voice,
And it told Thy love to me.
But I long to rise in the arms of faith
And be closer drawn to Thee.
FANNY CROSBY

Praying is not telling God what to do.
It's trusting that God knows what to do.
STORMIE OMARTIAN

More from God's Word

In quietness and in confidence shall be your strength.
ISAIAH 30:15 KJV

Listen, listen to me, and eat what is good,
and your soul will delight in the richest of fare.
Give ear and come to me; hear me, that your soul may live.
ISAIAH 55:2–3 NIV

Rest in the LORD, and wait patiently for Him.
PSALM 37:7 NKJV

The one who is from God listens to God's words.
This is why you don't listen, because you are not from God.
JOHN 8:47 HCSB

Be silent before Me.
ISAIAH 41:1 HCSB

A Timely Tip

If you want to have a meaningful conversation with God, don't make Him shout. Instead, go to a quiet place and listen. If you keep listening long enough and carefully enough, the Lord will talk directly to you.

67
LOVE

And now abide faith, hope, love, these three;
but the greatest of these is love.
1 CORINTHIANS 13:13 NKJV

God is love, and He intends that we share His love with the world. But He won't force us to be loving and kind. He places that responsibility squarely on our shoulders.

Love, like everything else in this world, begins and ends with God, but the middle part belongs to us. The Creator gives each of us the opportunity to be kind, to be courteous, and to be loving. He gives each of us the chance to obey the Golden Rule, or to make up our own rules as we go. If we obey God's instructions, we're secure, but if we do otherwise, we suffer.

Christ's words are clear: "'Love the Lord your God with all your heart and with all your soul and with all your mind.' This is the first and greatest commandment. And the second is like it: 'Love your neighbor as yourself.' All the Law and the Prophets hang on these two commandments" (Matthew 22:37–40 NIV). We are commanded to love the One who first loved us and then to share His love with the world. And the next move is always ours.

The vast ocean of Love cannot be measured or explained,
but it can be experienced.

SARAH YOUNG

Line by line, moment by moment, special times
are etched into our memories in the permanent ink
of everlasting love in our relationships.

GLORIA GAITHER

You can't really love other people well
unless you are at home in your own soul.
You will simply be too afraid.

PAULA RINEHART

When we do little acts of kindness
that make life more bearable for someone else,
we are walking in love as the Bible commands us.

BARBARA JOHNSON

A bird does not know it can fly before it uses its wings.
We learn God's love in our hearts as soon as we act upon it.

CORRIE TEN BOOM

More from God's Word

A new commandment I give unto you,
that ye love one another; as I have loved you,
that ye also love one another.
JOHN 13:34 KJV

Beloved, if God so loved us,
we ought also to love one another.
1 JOHN 4:11 KJV

Love is patient, love is kind.
Love does not envy, is not boastful, is not conceited.
1 CORINTHIANS 13:4 HCSB

Above all, love each other deeply,
because love covers a multitude of sins.
1 PETER 4:8 NIV

And we have known and believed the love
that God has for us. God is love, and he who abides
in love abides in God, and God in him.
1 JOHN 4:16 NKJV

A Timely Tip

Be creative. There are many ways to say, "I love you." Find them. Use them. And keep using them.

68

LOVING GOD

He said to him, "Love the Lord your God with all your heart,
with all your soul, and with all your mind.
This is the greatest and most important commandment."
MATTHEW 22:37–38 HCSB

The Bible teaches us to love God with all our hearts. But sometimes we fall short of the mark. Sometimes, despite our best intentions, we become embittered with ourselves, with our neighbors, or with our Creator.

If we are to please God, we must cleanse ourselves of the negative feelings that separate us from others and from Him. So today and every day, fill your heart with love. Don't yield to bitterness. And, praise the Son of God who, in His infinite wisdom, made love His greatest commandment. Put God first in your life and in your heart. He deserves your adoration, and you deserve the experience of giving it to Him.

*A wholehearted love for God looks to Him through His Word
and prayer, always watching and waiting, ever ready to do all
that He says, prepared to act on His expressed desires.*

ELIZABETH GEORGE

*Conditions are always changing; therefore,
I must not be dependent upon conditions.
What matters supremely is my soul and my relationship to God.*

CORRIE TEN BOOM

*Delighting thyself in the Lord is the sudden realization
that He has become the desire of your heart.*

BETH MOORE

*Loving Him means the thankful acceptance
of all things that His love has appointed.*

ELISABETH ELLIOT

*Joy is a by-product not of happy circumstances,
education, or talent, but of a healthy relationship with God
and a determination to love Him no matter what.*

BARBARA JOHNSON

More from God's Word

We love him, because he first loved us.
1 JOHN 4:19 KJV

This is love for God: to obey his commands.
1 JOHN 5:3 NIV

We know that all things work together for the good of those who love God: those who are called according to His purpose.
ROMANS 8:28 HCSB

God is Spirit, and those who worship Him must worship in spirit and truth.
JOHN 4:24 HCSB

I love the LORD, for he heard my voice; he heard my cry for mercy.
PSALM 116:1 NIV

A Timely Tip

Express yourself. If you sincerely love God, don't be too bashful to tell Him so. And while you're at it, don't be too bashful to tell other people about your feelings. If you love the Lord, say so loudly and often.

69

MATERIALISM

*No one can serve two masters. For you will hate one
and love the other, or be devoted to one and despise the other.
You cannot serve God and be enslaved to money.*

LUKE 16:13 NLT

The world's message is abundantly clear: collect enough material possessions, and you'll be happy. But God's Word warns against such shallow thinking. The Bible teaches us that the love of money—and the love of things that money can buy—is a trap that inevitably leads to disappointment, to disillusionment, and, ultimately, to destruction.

In the course of a well-lived life, material possessions play a surprisingly small role. Of course, poverty is stressful, and we all need the basic necessities of life, but once we meet those needs for ourselves and our loved ones, the piling up of possessions may create unexpected headaches.

Our real riches, of course, cannot be purchased at the mall, or anywhere else, for that matter. Our real riches are the spiritual kind. So if you find yourself fretting about money, or the things money can buy, perhaps it's time to reorder your priorities. And, it's time to begin storing up riches that are destined to endure throughout eternity—the spiritual kind.

*The more we stuff ourselves with material pleasures,
the less we seem to appreciate life.*
BARBARA JOHNSON

*It's sobering to contemplate how much time,
effort, sacrifice, compromise, and attention
we give to acquiring and increasing our supply
of something that is totally insignificant in eternity.*
ANNE GRAHAM LOTZ

*Greed is enslaving. The more you have,
the more you want—until eventually avarice consumes you.*
KAY ARTHUR

*As faithful stewards of what we have,
ought we not to give earnest thought
to our staggering surplus?*
ELISABETH ELLIOT

Why is love of gold more potent than love of souls?
LOTTIE MOON

More from God's Word

For where your treasure is, there your heart will be also.
LUKE 12:34 HCSB

We brought nothing into the world, so we can take nothing out.
But, if we have food and clothes, we will be satisfied with that.
1 TIMOTHY 6:7–8 NCV

Your life should be free from the love of money.
Be satisfied with what you have, for He Himself has said,
I will never leave you or forsake you.
HEBREWS 13:5 HCSB

Do not love the world or the things that belong to the world.
If anyone loves the world, love for the Father is not in him.
1 JOHN 2:15 HCSB

There is one who makes himself rich, yet has nothing;
and one who makes himself poor, yet has great riches.
PROVERBS 13:7 NKJV

A Timely Tip

The world wants you to believe that "money and stuff" can buy happiness. Don't believe it! Genuine happiness comes not from money, but from the things that money can't buy—starting, of course, with your relationship with God and His only begotten Son.

70

MIRACLES

Is anything too hard for the LORD?
GENESIS 18:14 NKJV

God's power has no limitations. He is not restrained by the laws of nature because He created those laws. At any time, in any place, under any set of circumstances, He can accomplish anything He chooses. The things that seem miraculous to us are, to Him, expressions of His power and His love.

Do you expect God to work miracles in your own life? You should. From the moment He created our universe out of nothingness, the Lord has made a habit of doing miraculous things. And He's still working miracles today.

With God nothing is impossible. His wondrous works come in all shapes and sizes, so keep your eyes and your heart open. Somewhere, a miracle is about to happen, and it might just happen to you.

God specializes in things thought impossible.
CATHERINE MARSHALL

Are you looking for a miracle?
If you keep your eyes wide open and trust in God,
you won't have to look very far.
MARIE T. FREEMAN

God's faithfulness and grace
make the impossible possible.
SHEILA WALSH

Faith means believing in realities
that go beyond sense and sight.
It is the awareness of unseen
divine realities all around you.
JONI EARECKSON TADA

I could go through this day oblivious
to the miracles all around me
or I could tune in and "enjoy."
GLORIA GAITHER

More from God's Word

*God confirmed the message by giving signs
and wonders and various miracles and gifts
of the Holy Spirit whenever he chose.*
HEBREWS 2:4 NLT

*You are the God of great wonders!
You demonstrate your awesome power among the nations.*
PSALM 77:14 NLT

*No eye has seen, no ear has heard, no mind has conceived
what God has prepared for those who love him.*
1 CORINTHIANS 2:9 NIV

*And Jesus looking upon them saith, With men it is impossible,
but not with God: for with God all things are possible.*
MARK 10:27 KJV

For with God nothing shall be impossible.
LUKE 1:37 KJV

A Timely Tip

Never be afraid to hope—or to ask—for a miracle.

71
OBEDIENCE

Now by this we know that we know Him,
if we keep His commandments.
1 JOHN 2:3 NKJV

God's instructions to mankind are contained in a book like no other: the holy Bible. When we obey God's commandments and listen carefully to the conscience He has placed in our hearts, we are secure. But if we disobey our Creator, if we choose to ignore the teachings and the warnings of His Word, we do so at great peril.

Susanna Wesley said, "There are two things to do about the gospel: believe it and behave it." Her words serve as a powerful reminder that, as Christians, we are called to take God's promises seriously and to live in accordance with His teachings.

God gave us His commandments for a reason: so that we might obey them and be blessed. Yet we live in a world that presents us with countless temptations to stray far from His path. It is our responsibility to resist those temptations with vigor. Obedience isn't just the best way to experience the full measure of God's blessings; it's the only way.

You may not always see immediate results,
but all God wants is your obedience and faithfulness.
VONETTE BRIGHT

To yield to God means to belong to God,
and to belong to God means to have all His infinite power.
To belong to God means to have all.
HANNAH WHITALL SMITH

Obedience is a foundational stepping-stone
on the path of God's will.
ELIZABETH GEORGE

Rejoicing is a matter of obedience to God—
an obedience that will start you
on the road to peace and contentment.
KAY ARTHUR

Obedience goes before our hearts and carries them
where they would not normally go.
PAULA RINEHART

More from God's Word

We must obey God rather than men.
ACTS 5:29 NASB

Trust in the LORD with all your heart,
and lean not on your own understanding;
in all your ways acknowledge Him,
and He shall direct your paths.
PROVERBS 3:5–6 NKJV

Teach me, O LORD, the way of Your statutes,
and I shall observe it to the end.
PSALM 119:33 NASB

Praise the LORD! Happy are those who respect the LORD,
who want what he commands.
PSALM 112:1 NCV

But prove yourselves doers of the word,
and not merely hearers who delude themselves.
JAMES 1:22 NASB

A Timely Tip

Obedience leads to spiritual growth. Anne Graham Lotz correctly observed, "If you want to discover your spiritual gifts, start obeying God. As you serve Him, you will find that He has given you the gifts that are necessary to follow through in obedience."

72

OPPORTUNITIES

*Remember ye not the former things, neither consider
the things of old. Behold, I will do a new thing.*
ISAIAH 43:18–19 KJV

As you consider the trajectory of your career—and as you consider
your opportunities for service—do you see possibilities, opportunities, and blessings from above? Or do you focus on stumbling
blocks instead of stepping stones?

If you're consistently looking for opportunities, you'll discover
that opportunities have a way of turning up in the most unexpected
places. But, if you've acquired the unfortunate habit of looking for
problems instead of possibilities, you'll find that troubles have a
way of turning up in unexpected places, too.

Since you're likely to find what you're looking for, why not look
for opportunities? They're out there. And the rest is up to you.

*Each day is God's gift of a fresh unspoiled opportunity
to live according to His priorities.*
ELIZABETH GEORGE

*Every day we live is a priceless gift of God,
loaded with possibilities to learn something new,
to gain fresh insights.*
DALE EVANS ROGERS

*God specializes in things fresh and firsthand.
His plans for you this year may outshine those of the past.
He's prepared to fill your days with reasons to give Him praise.*
JONI EARECKSON TADA

*If all things are possible with God,
then all things are possible to him who believes in Him.*
CORRIE TEN BOOM

*Sometimes new opportunity means new opposition.
Not everything God asks us to do will be comfortable.*
JOYCE MEYER

MORE FROM GOD'S WORD

*As it is written: What eye did not see and ear did not hear,
and what never entered the human mind—
God prepared this for those who love Him.*
1 CORINTHIANS 2:9 HCSB

I can do all things through Christ which strengtheneth me.
PHILIPPIANS 4:13 KJV

*Whenever we have the opportunity, we should do good
to everyone—especially to those in the family of faith.*
GALATIANS 6:10 NLT

I remind you to fan into flame the gift of God.
2 TIMOTHY 1:6 NIV

*But those who wait on the LORD shall renew their strength;
they shall mount up with wings like eagles, they shall run
and not be weary, they shall walk and not faint.*
ISAIAH 40:31 NKJV

A TIMELY TIP

God gives us opportunities for a reason: to use them. And, God wants you to make the most of all the opportunities He sends your way. Now.

73

OPTIMISM

The LORD is my light and my salvation—
whom should I fear? The LORD is the stronghold of my life—
of whom should I be afraid?

PSALM 27:1 HCSB

Christians have every reason to be optimistic about life. As Kay Arthur observed, "Joy is available to all who seek His riches. The key to joy is found in the person of Jesus Christ and in His will." But sometimes rejoicing is the last thing on our minds. Sometimes we fall prey to worry, frustration, anxiety, or sheer exhaustion . . . and our hearts become heavy. What's needed is plenty of rest, a large dose of perspective, and God's healing touch, but not necessarily in that order.

Jesus offers us abundance and joy, but He doesn't force abundance and joy upon us; we must claim these gifts for ourselves. Today, why not claim the joy that is rightfully yours in Christ? Why not take time to celebrate God's glorious creation? When you do so, you will think optimistically about yourself and your world, and you can then share your optimism with others. You'll be better for it, and so will they.

So, the next time you find yourself dwelling upon the negative aspects of your life, refocus your attention on things positive. The next time you find yourself falling prey to the blight of pessimism, stop yourself and turn your thoughts around. The next time you're tempted to waste valuable time gossiping or complaining, resist those temptations with all your might. And remember: You'll never complain your way to the top, so don't waste your breath.

It never hurts your eyesight to look on the bright side of things.
BARBARA JOHNSON

The Christian lifestyle is not one of legalistic do's and don'ts, but one that is positive, attractive, and joyful.
VONETTE BRIGHT

Stop thinking wishfully and start living hopefully.
EMILIE BARNES

Make the least of all that goes and the most of all that comes. Don't regret what is past. Cherish what you have. Look forward to all that is to come. And most important of all, rely moment by moment on Jesus Christ.
GIGI GRAHAM TCHIVIDJIAN

We may run, walk, stumble, drive, or fly, but let us never lose sight of the reason for the journey, or miss a chance to see a rainbow on the way.
GLORIA GAITHER

More from God's Word

Make me to hear joy and gladness.
PSALM 51:8 KJV

*"I say this because I know what I am planning for you,"
says the LORD. "I have good plans for you, not plans to hurt
you. I will give you hope and a good future."*
JEREMIAH 29:11 NCV

*But if we look forward to something we don't yet have,
we must wait patiently and confidently.*
ROMANS 8:25 NLT

*This hope we have as an anchor of the soul,
a hope both sure and steadfast.*
HEBREWS 6:19 NASB

*Let us hold on to the confession of our hope without wavering,
for He who promised is faithful.*
HEBREWS 10:23 HCSB

A Timely Tip

Optimism pays. Pessimism does not. Guard your thoughts and your words accordingly. Today (and every day), it's time to count your blessings and to think optimistically about your future.

74
PAST

Do not remember the former things, nor consider the things of old. Behold, I will do a new thing.
ISAIAH 43:18–19 NKJV

Since we can't change the pains and disappointments of the past, why do so many of us insist upon replaying them over and over again in our minds? Perhaps it's because we can't find it in our hearts to forgive the people who have hurt us. Being mere mortals, we seek revenge, not reconciliation, and we harbor hatred in our hearts, sometimes for decades.

Reinhold Niebuhr composed a simple verse that came to be known as the Serenity Prayer: "God, grant me the serenity to accept the things I cannot change, the courage to change the things I can, and the wisdom to know the difference." Obviously, we cannot change the past. It is what it was and forever will be. The present, of course, is a different matter.

Today is filled with opportunities to live, to love, to work, to play, and to celebrate life. If we sincerely wish to build a better tomorrow, we can start building it today, in the present moment. So, if you've endured a difficult past, accept it, learn from it, and forgive everybody, including yourself. Once you've made peace with your past, don't spend too much time there. Instead, live in the precious present, where opportunities abound and change is still possible.

We set our eyes on the finish line,
forgetting the past, and straining toward
the mark of spiritual maturity and fruitfulness.
VONETTE BRIGHT

Shake the dust from your past,
and move forward in His promises.
KAY ARTHUR

Our yesterdays teach us how to savor
our todays and tomorrows.
PATSY CLAIRMONT

You cannot change the past,
but you can control your own attitude.
BARBARA JOHNSON

Our past experiences may have made
us the way we are, but we don't have to stay that way.
JOYCE MEYER

More from God's Word

*One thing I do, forgetting those things which are behind
and reaching forward to those things which are ahead,
I press toward the goal for the prize
of the upward call of God in Christ Jesus.*
PHILIPPIANS 3:13–14 NKJV

*Your old sinful self has died, and your new life
is kept with Christ in God.*
COLOSSIANS 3:3 NCV

*Have mercy on me, O God, according to your unfailing love;
according to your great compassion blot out my transgressions.
Wash away all my iniquity and cleanse me from my sin.*
PSALM 51:1–2 NIV

*He restoreth my soul: he leadeth me
in the paths of righteousness for his name's sake.*
PSALM 23:3 KJV

*And He who sits on the throne said,
"Behold, I am making all things new."*
REVELATION 21:5 NASB

A Timely Tip

Once you accept the past—and make peace with it—you are
free to live joyfully in the present. And that's precisely what you
should do.

75

PATIENCE

A person's wisdom yields patience;
it is to one's glory to overlook an offense.
PROVERBS 19:11 NIV

We human beings are, by our very nature, impatient. We are impatient with others, impatient with ourselves, and impatient with our Creator. We want things to happen according to our own timetables, but our heavenly Father may have other plans. That's why we must learn the art of patience.

Psalm 37:7 commands us to "rest in the LORD, and wait patiently for Him" (NKJV). But, for most of us, waiting patiently for Him is difficult. Why? Because we are fallible people who seek solutions to our problems today, if not sooner. Still, God instructs us to wait patiently for His plans to unfold, and that's exactly what we should do.

So the next time you find yourself drumming your fingers as you wait for a quick resolution to the challenges of everyday living, take a deep breath and ask God for patience. Be still before your heavenly Father and trust His timetable: it's the peaceful way to live.

Waiting is the hardest kind of work,
but God knows best,
and we may joyfully leave all in His hands.
LOTTIE MOON

Wisdom always waits for the right time to act,
while emotion always pushes for action right now.
JOYCE MEYER

How do you wait upon the Lord?
First you must learn to sit at His feet
and take time to listen to His words.
KAY ARTHUR

When we read of the great Biblical leaders,
we see that it was not uncommon for God
to ask them to wait, not just a day or two,
but for years, until God was ready for them to act.
GLORIA GAITHER

We must learn to wait.
There is grace supplied to the one who waits.
LETTIE COWMAN

More from God's Word

Patience of spirit is better than haughtiness of spirit.
ECCLESIASTES 7:8 NASB

But if we hope for what we do not yet have,
we wait for it patiently.
ROMANS 8:25 NIV

Better to be patient than powerful;
better to have self-control than to conquer a city.
PROVERBS 16:32 NLT

Be joyful in hope, patient in affliction,
faithful in prayer.
ROMANS 12:12 NIV

The LORD is good to those who depend on him,
to those who search for him.
So it is good to wait quietly for salvation from the LORD.
LAMENTATIONS 3:25–26 NLT

A Timely Tip

Patience pays. Impatience costs. When you learn to be a more patient person, you'll make your world—and your heart—a better place.

76
PEACE

Peace I leave with you, My peace I give to you;
not as the world gives do I give to you.
Let not your heart be troubled, neither let it be afraid.
JOHN 14:27 NKJV

Peace. It's such a beautiful word. It conveys images of serenity, contentment, and freedom from the trials and tribulations of everyday existence. Peace means freedom from conflict, freedom from inner turmoil, and freedom from worry. Peace is such a beautiful concept that advertisers and marketers attempt to sell it with images of relaxed vacationers lounging on the beach or happy senior citizens celebrating on the golf course. But contrary to the implied claims of modern media, real peace, genuine peace, isn't for sale. At any price.

Have you discovered the genuine peace that can be yours through Christ? Or are you still scurrying after the illusion of peace that the world promises but cannot deliver? If you've turned things over to Jesus, you'll be blessed now and forever. So what are you waiting for? Let Him rule your heart and your thoughts, beginning now. When you do, you'll experience the peace that only He can give.

In the center of a hurricane
there is absolute quiet and peace.
There is no safer place than
in the center of the will of God.

CORRIE TEN BOOM

Prayer guards hearts and minds
and causes God to bring peace out of chaos.

BETH MOORE

Peace does not mean to be in a place where
there is no noise, trouble, or hard work.
Peace means to be in the midst of all those things
and still be calm in your heart.

CATHERINE MARSHALL

The fruit of our placing all things in God's hands
is the presence of His abiding peace in our hearts.

HANNAH WHITALL SMITH

When we do what is right,
we have contentment, peace, and happiness.

BEVERLY LaHAYE

More from God's Word

He Himself is our peace.
EPHESIANS 2:14 NASB

*But the fruit of the Spirit is love, joy, peace,
patience, kindness, goodness, faith, gentleness, self-control.
Against such things there is no law.*
GALATIANS 5:22–23 HCSB

*The peace of God, which passeth all understanding,
shall keep your hearts and minds through Christ Jesus.*
PHILIPPIANS 4:7 KJV

*"I will give peace, real peace, to those far and near,
and I will heal them," says the LORD.*
ISAIAH 57:19 NCV

*These things I have spoken to you, that in Me
you may have peace. In the world you will have tribulation;
but be of good cheer, I have overcome the world.*
JOHN 16:33 NKJV

A Timely Tip

Sometimes peace can be a scarce commodity in a noisy, complicated, twenty-first century world. But God's peace is always available when you turn everything over to Him.

77

PERSEVERANCE

Let us not become weary in doing good,
for at the proper time we will reap
a harvest if we do not give up.
GALATIANS 6:9 NIV

Occasionally, good things happen with little or no effort. Somebody wins the lottery, or inherits a fortune, or stumbles onto a financial bonanza by being at the right place at the right time. But more often than not, good things happen to people who work hard, and keep working hard, when just about everybody else has gone home or given up.

Calvin Coolidge observed, "Nothing in the world can take the place of persistence. Talent will not; genius will not; education will not. Persistence and determination alone are omnipotent." President Coolidge was right. Perseverance pays.

Every marathon has a finish line, and so does yours. So keep putting one foot in front of the other, pray for strength, and don't give up. Whether you realize it or not, you're up to the challenge if you persevere. And with God's help, that's exactly what you'll do.

We are all on our way somewhere.
We'll get there if we just keep going.
BARBARA JOHNSON

If things are tough, remember that every flower that ever
bloomed had to go through a whole lot of dirt to get there.
BARBARA JOHNSON

Failure is one of life's most powerful teachers.
How we handle our failures determines whether
we're going to simply "get by" in life or "press on."
BETH MOORE

Are you a Christian? If you are,
how can you be hopeless?
Are you so depressed by the greatness
of your problems that you have given up all hope?
Instead of giving up, would you patiently endure?
Would you focus on Christ
until you are so preoccupied with Him alone
that you fall prostrate before Him?
ANNE GRAHAM LOTZ

More from God's Word

But as for you, be strong; don't be discouraged,
for your work has a reward.
2 Chronicles 15:7 HCSB

Finishing is better than starting.
Patience is better than pride.
Ecclesiastes 7:8 NLT

We are hard-pressed on every side, yet not crushed;
we are perplexed, but not in despair.
2 Corinthians 4:8 NKJV

For you have need of endurance, so that when you have done
the will of God, you may receive what was promised.
Hebrews 10:36 NASB

So let us run the race that is before us and never give up.
We should remove from our lives anything that would
get in the way and the sin that so easily holds us back.
Hebrews 12:1 NCV

A Timely Tip

Life is, at times, difficult. When you are tested, don't quit at the first sign of trouble. Instead, call upon God. He can give you the strength to persevere, and that's exactly what you should ask Him to do.

78

PERSPECTIVE

So teach us to number our days,
that we may gain a heart of wisdom.
PSALM 90:12 NKJV

Life in the twenty-first century can be busy and complicated. Amid the rush and crush of the daily grind, it's easy to lose perspective, it's easy to become frustrated, and it's easy to lose sight of the real reason God put us here.

When our world seems to be spinning out of control, we can regain perspective by slowing ourselves down and then turning our thoughts and prayers toward the Creator of the universe. When we do, He calms our spirits and restores our sense of perspective.

Do you carve out quiet moments each day to praise your Creator? You should. The familiar words of Psalm 46:10 remind us to "Be still, and know that I am God" (NKJV). When we do, we encounter the awesome presence of our loving heavenly Father, and we are blessed beyond words. But, if we ignore the presence of our Creator, we rob ourselves of His perspective, His peace, and His joy.

Today and every day, make time to be still before God. When you do, you can face the day's complications with the wisdom and power that only He can provide.

When you are experiencing the challenges of life,
perspective is everything.
JONI EARECKSON TADA

When we look at the individual parts of our lives,
some things appear unfair and unpleasant.
When we take them out of the context of the big picture,
we easily drift into the attitude that we deserve better,
and the tumble down into the pit of pride begins.
SUSAN HUNT

Like a shadow declining swiftly . . . away . . .
like the dew of the morning gone with
the heat of the day; like the wind in the treetops,
like a wave of the sea, so are our lives
on earth when seen in light of eternity.
RUTH BELL GRAHAM

Earthly fears are no fears at all. Answer
the big questions of eternity,
and the little questions of life fall into perspective.
MAX LUCADO

The proper perspective creates within us a spirit of reaching
outside of ourselves with joy and enthusiasm.
LUCI SWINDOLL

More from God's Word

*Joyful is the person who finds wisdom
the one who gains understanding.*
PROVERBS 3:13 NLT

*The one who acquires good sense loves himself;
one who safeguards understanding finds success.*
PROVERBS 19:8 HCSB

If you teach the wise, they will get knowledge.
PROVERBS 21:11 NCV

*Since you have been raised to new life with Christ,
set your sights on the realities of heaven, where Christ sits
in the place of honor at God's right hand.*
COLOSSIANS 3:1 NLT

*Trust in the Lord with all your heart,
and lean not on your own understanding;
in all your ways acknowledge Him,
and He shall direct your paths.*
PROVERBS 3:5–6 NKJV

A Timely Tip

Your life is an integral part of God's grand plan. So don't become unduly upset over the minor inconveniences of life, and don't worry too much about today's setbacks—they're temporary.

79

PLEASING GOD

For merely listening to the law doesn't make us right with God.
It is obeying the law that makes us right in his sight.
ROMANS 2:13 NLT

Sometimes, because you're an imperfect human being, you may become so wrapped up in meeting society's expectations that you fail to focus on God's expectations. To do so is a mistake of major proportions—don't make it. Instead, seek God's guidance in every aspect of your life. And, when it comes to matters of conscience, seek approval not from your peers, but from your Creator.

Whom will you try to please today: God or mankind? Your primary obligation is not to please imperfect friends or casual acquaintances. Your obligation is to meet the Lord's expectations. So, turn your concerns over to Him—prayerfully, earnestly, and often. Then, listen for His answers, and trust the answers He gives.

Make God's will the focus of your life day by day.
If you seek to please Him and Him alone,
you'll find yourself satisfied with life.
KAY ARTHUR

Prayer is a habit. Worship is a habit.
Kindness is a habit. And if you want to please God,
you'd better make sure that these habits are your habits.
MARIE T. FREEMAN

God is not hard to please.
He does not expect us to be absolutely perfect.
He just expects us to keep moving toward Him
and believing in Him, letting Him work with us
to bring us into conformity to His will and ways.
JOYCE MEYER

You may not always see immediate results,
but all God wants is your obedience and faithfulness.
VONETTE BRIGHT

A prayerful heart and an obedient heart will learn,
very slowly and not without sorrow,
to stake everything on God Himself.
ELISABETH ELLIOT

MORE FROM GOD'S WORD

Our only goal is to please God whether we live here or there,
because we must all stand before Christ to be judged.
2 CORINTHIANS 5:9–10 NCV

Give to the LORD the glory due His name;
bring an offering, and come into His courts.
PSALM 96:8 NKJV

But prove yourselves doers of the word,
and not merely hearers who delude themselves.
JAMES 1:22 NASB

It is impossible to please God without faith.
Anyone who wants to come to him must believe that
God exists and that he rewards those who sincerely seek him.
HEBREWS 11:6 NLT

A TIMELY TIP

Being obedient to God means that you can't always please other people. So focus, first and foremost, on your relationship with the Creator. When you do, you'll find that every other relationship and every other aspect of your life will be more fulfilling.

80

PLEASING PEOPLE

For am I now trying to win the favor of people, or God?
Or am I striving to please people? If I were still trying
to please people, I would not be a slave of Christ.
GALATIANS 1:10 HCSB

If you're like most women, you seek the admiration of your friends, your neighbors, your coworkers, and, most importantly, your family members. But the eagerness to please others should never overshadow your eagerness to please God.

Life is a series of decisions and choices. Each day, we make countless decisions that can bring us closer to God . . . or not. When we live according to God's commandments, we earn for ourselves the abundance and peace that He intends for our lives. But when we concern ourselves more with pleasing others than with pleasing our Creator, we bring needless suffering upon ourselves and our families.

Would you like a time-tested formula for successful living? Here is a formula that is proven and true: Seek God's approval in every aspect of your life. Does this sound too simple? Perhaps it is simple, but it is also the only way to reap the marvelous riches that God has in store for you.

If pleasing people is your goal,
you will be enslaved to them.
People can be harsh taskmasters
when you give them this power over you.

SARAH YOUNG

It is comfortable to know that we are responsible
to God and not to man. It is a small matter
to be judged of man's judgement.

LOTTIE MOON

Stop determining your worth
and value by what other people say.
Be determined by what the Word of God says.

JOYCE MEYER

The major problem with letting others
define you is that it borders on idolatry.
Your concern to please others dampens
your desire to please your Creator.

SARAH YOUNG

You will get untold flak for prioritizing God's
revealed and present will for your life over man's,
but, boy, is it worth it.

BETH MOORE

More from God's Word

The fear of man is a snare,
but the one who trusts in the LORD is protected.
PROVERBS 29:25 HCSB

My son, if sinners entice you,
don't be persuaded.
PROVERBS 1:10 HCSB

It is better to take refuge in the LORD than to trust in man.
PSALM 118:8 HCSB

Keep your eyes focused on what is right.
Keep looking straight ahead to what is good.
PROVERBS 4:25 ICB

Do not be unequally yoked together with unbelievers.
For what fellowship has righteousness with lawlessness?
And what communion has light with darkness?
2 CORINTHIANS 6:14 NKJV

A Timely Tip

If you are burdened with a "people-pleasing" personality, out-grow it. Realize that you can't please all of the people all of the time, nor should you attempt to.

81

PRAISE

Let everything that breathes praise the LORD. Hallelujah!
PSALM 150:6 HCSB

Too many of us, even well-intentioned believers, tend to "compartmentalize" our waking hours into a few familiar categories: work, rest, play, family time, and worship. As creatures of habit, we may find ourselves praising God only at particular times of the day or the week. But praise for our Creator should never be reserved for mealtimes, or bedtimes, or church. Instead, we should praise God all day, every day, to the greatest extent we can, with thanksgiving in our hearts and with a song on our lips.

Worship and praise should be woven into the fabric of everything we do; they should not be relegated to a weekly visit to church on Sunday morning. So today and every day, find time to lift your prayers to God, and thank Him for all that He has done. Every time you notice a gift from the Giver of all things good, praise Him. His works are marvelous, His gifts are beyond understanding, and His love endures forever.

*Nothing we do is more powerful
or more life-changing than praising God.*
STORMIE OMARTIAN

*Our God is the sovereign Creator of the universe!
He loves us as His own children
and has provided every good thing we have;
He is worthy of our praise every moment.*
SHIRLEY DOBSON

Preoccupy my thoughts with Your praise beginning today.
JONI EARECKSON TADA

*Two wings are necessary to lift our souls
toward God: prayer and praise.
Prayer asks. Praise accepts the answer.*
LETTIE COWMAN

*Words fail to express my love for this holy Book,
my gratitude for its author, for His love and goodness.
How shall I thank Him for it?*
LOTTIE MOON

More from God's Word

Great is the LORD! He is most worthy of praise!
No one can measure his greatness.
PSALM 145:3 NLT

At the name of Jesus every knee should bow,
of things in heaven, and things in earth,
and things under the earth; and that every tongue should
confess that Jesus Christ is Lord, to the glory of God the Father.
PHILIPPIANS 2:10–11 KJV

In everything give thanks; for this
is the will of God in Christ Jesus for you.
1 THESSALONIANS 5:18 NKJV

The LORD is my strength and my song;
He has become my salvation.
EXODUS 15:2 HCSB

From the rising of the sun to its setting,
the name of the LORD is to be praised.
PSALM 113:3 NASB

A Timely Tip

All of your talents and opportunities come from God. Give Him the thanks, and give Him the glory. And remember: the appropriate moment to praise God is always this one.

82

PRAYER

Rejoice always, pray without ceasing, in everything give thanks;
for this is the will of God in Christ Jesus for you.
1 THESSALONIANS 5:16–18 NKJV

This troubled world desperately needs your prayers, and so does your family. When you weave the habit of prayer into the very fabric of your day, you invite God to become a partner in every aspect of your life. When you consult God on an hourly basis, you avail yourself of His wisdom, His strength, and His love. And, because God answers prayers according to His perfect timetable, your petitions to Him will transform your family, your world, and yourself.

Today, turn everything over to your Creator in prayer. Instead of worrying about your next decision, decide to let God lead the way. Don't limit your prayers to meals or to bedtime. Pray constantly about things great and small. God is listening, and He wants to hear from you. Now.

What God gives in answer to our prayers
will always be the thing we most urgently need,
and it will always be sufficient.
ELISABETH ELLIOT

Your family and friends need your prayers
and you need theirs. And God wants to hear those prayers.
So what are you waiting for?
MARIE T. FREEMAN

God says we don't need to be anxious about anything;
we just need to pray about everything.
STORMIE OMARTIAN

We must leave it to God to answer our prayers
in His own wisest way. Sometimes, we are so impatient
and think that God does not answer. God always answers!
He never fails! Be still. Abide in Him.
LETTIE COWMAN

Are you weak? Weary? Confused? Troubled?
Pressured? How is your relationship with God?
Is it held in its place of priority? I believe the greater
the pressure, the greater your need for time alone with Him.
KAY ARTHUR

More from God's Word

*I desire therefore that the men pray everywhere,
lifting up holy hands, without wrath and doubting.*
1 Timothy 2:8 NKJV

*Confess your trespasses to one another,
and pray for one another, that you may be healed.
The effective, fervent prayer of a righteous man avails much.*
James 5:16 NKJV

Is anyone among you suffering? He should pray.
James 5:13 HCSB

*And whenever you stand praying, if you have anything
against anyone, forgive him, so that your
Father in heaven may also forgive you your wrongdoing.*
Mark 11:25 HCSB

*Ask, and it shall be given to you; seek, and you shall find;
knock, and it shall be opened to you.
For every one who asks receives, and he who seeks finds,
and to him who knocks it will be opened.*
Matthew 7:7–8 NASB

A Timely Tip

God does not answer all of our prayers in the affirmative. When we are disappointed by the realities of life here on earth, we should remember that our prayers are always answered by an all-knowing God, and that we must trust Him, whatever the answer.

83

PRIDE

A patient spirit is better than a proud spirit.
ECCLESIASTES 7:8 HCSB

As fallible human beings, we have so much to be humble about. Why, then, is humility such a difficult trait for us to master? Precisely because we are fallible human beings. Yet if we are to grow and mature as Christians, we must strive to give credit where credit is due, starting, of course, with God and His only begotten Son.

As Christians, we have been refashioned and saved by Jesus Christ, and that salvation came not because of our own good works but because of God's grace. Thus, we are not "self-made," we are "God-made," and we are "Christ-saved." How, then, can we be boastful? The answer, of course, is that, if we are honest with ourselves and with our God, we simply can't be boastful. We must, instead, be eternally grateful and exceedingly humble. Humility, however, is not easy for most of us. All too often, we are tempted to say, "Look at me; look what I did!" But, in the quiet moments when we search the depths of our own hearts, we know better. Whatever "it" is, God did that. And He deserves the credit.

If you know who you are in Christ,
your personal ego is not an issue.
BETH MOORE

That's what I love about serving God.
In His eyes, there are no little people . . .
because there are no big people.
We are all on the same playing field.
We all start at square one.
No one has it better than the other,
or possesses unfair advantage.
JONI EARECKSON TADA

That some of my hymns have been
dictated by the blessed Holy Spirit I have no doubt;
and that others have been the result of deep meditation
I know to be true; but that the poet has any right
to claim special merit for himself is certainly presumptuous.
FANNY CROSBY

All kindness and good deeds, we must keep silent.
The result will be an inner reservoir of personality power.
CATHERINE MARSHALL

We are never stronger than the moment
we admit we are weak.
BETH MOORE

More from God's Word

God resists the proud, but gives grace to the humble.
JAMES 4:6 HCSB

For those who exalt themselves will be humbled,
and those who humble themselves will be exalted.
MATTHEW 23:12 NIV

You save the humble,
but you bring down those who are proud.
2 SAMUEL 22:28 NCV

When pride comes, disgrace follows,
but with humility comes wisdom.
PROVERBS 11:2 HCSB

Do nothing out of rivalry or conceit,
but in humility consider others
as more important than yourselves.
PHILIPPIANS 2:3 HCSB

A Timely Tip

God favors the humble just as surely as He disciplines the proud.
Humility leads to contentment; pride doesn't. Act accordingly.

84

RENEWAL

Therefore, if anyone is in Christ,
he is a new creation; old things have passed away;
behold, all things have become new.
2 CORINTHIANS 5:17 NKJV

For busy citizens of the twenty-first century, it's easy to become overcommitted, overworked, and over-stressed. If we choose, we can be connected 24/7, sparing just enough time for a few hours' sleep each night. What we need is time to renew and recharge, but where can we find the time? We can—and should—find it with God.

God can renew your strength and restore your spirits if you let Him. But He won't force you to slow down, and He won't insist that you get enough sleep at night. He leaves those choices up to you.

If you're feeling chronically tired or discouraged, it's time to rearrange your schedule, turn off the TV, power down the phone, and spend quiet time with your Creator. He knows what you need, and He wants you to experience His peace and His love. He's ready, willing, and perfectly able to renew your strength and help you prioritize the items on your do-list if you ask Him. In fact, He's ready to hear your prayers right now. Please don't make Him wait.

He is the God of wholeness and restoration.
STORMIE OMARTIAN

God specializes in things fresh and firsthand.
His plans for you this year may outshine those of the past.
He's prepared to fill your days with reasons to give Him praise.
JONI EARECKSON TADA

When we reach the end of our strength,
wisdom, and personal resources,
we enter into the beginning of His glorious provisions.
PATSY CLAIRMONT

Each of us has something broken in our lives:
a broken promise, a broken dream, a broken marriage,
a broken heart. We must decide how we're going to deal
with our brokenness. We can wallow in self-pity or regret,
accomplishing nothing and having no fun or joy in our
circumstances; or we can determine with our will to take
a few risks, get out of our comfort zone, and see what God
will do to bring unexpected delight in our time of need.
LUCI SWINDOLL

In those desperate times when we feel like we don't
have an ounce of strength, He will gently pick up
our heads so that our eyes can behold something—
something that will keep His hope alive in us.
KATHY TROCCOLI

More from God's Word

You are being renewed in the spirit of your minds;
you put on the new self, the one created according to God's
likeness in righteousness and purity of the truth.
Ephesians 4:23–24 HCSB

Remember ye not the former things, neither consider
the things of old. Behold, I will do a new thing.
Isaiah 43:18–19 KJV

Those who hope in the LORD will renew their strength.
They will soar on wings like eagles; they will run
and not grow weary, they will walk and not be faint.
Isaiah 40:31 NIV

Finally, brothers, rejoice. Be restored, be encouraged,
be of the same mind, be at peace, and the God of love
and peace will be with you.
2 Corinthians 13:11 HCSB

Now the God of all grace, who called you
to His eternal glory in Christ Jesus, will personally
restore, establish, strengthen, and support you.
1 Peter 5:10 HCSB

A Timely Tip

God can make all things new, including you. When you are weak or worried, He can renew your spirit and restore your strength. Your job, of course, is to let Him.

85
REST

*Come unto me, all ye that labor and are heavy laden,
and I will give you rest.*
MATTHEW 11:28 KJV

You inhabit an interconnected world that never slows down and never shuts off. The world tempts you to stay up late watching the news, or surfing the Internet, or checking out social media, or gaming, or doing countless other activities that gobble up your time and distract you from more important tasks. But too much late-night screen time robs you of something you need very badly: sleep.

Are you going to bed at a reasonable hour and sleeping through the night? If so, you're both wise and blessed. But if you're staying up late with your eyes glued to a screen, you're putting your long-term health at risk. And, you're probably wasting time, too.

So, the next time you're tempted to engage in late-night time-wasting, resist the temptation. Instead, turn your thoughts and prayers to God. And when you're finished, turn off the lights and go to bed. You need rest more than you need entertainment.

Life is strenuous. See that your clock does not run down.
LETTIE COWMAN

Jesus taught us by example to get out
of the rat race and recharge our batteries.
BARBARA JOHNSON

Come, come, come unto Me,
Weary and sore distressed;
Come, come, come unto Me,
Come unto Me and rest.
FANNY CROSBY

Energy and time are limited entities.
Therefore, we need to use them wisely,
focusing on what is truly important.
SARAH YOUNG

Be still, and in the quiet moments,
listen to the voice of your heavenly Father.
His words can renew your spirit—
no one knows you and your needs like He does.
JANET L. WEAVER SMITH

More from God's Word

Take My yoke upon you and learn from Me,
because I am gentle and humble in heart,
and you will find rest for your souls.
For My yoke is easy and My burden is light.
Matthew 11:29–30 HCSB

The Lord shall give thee rest from thy sorrow,
and from thy fear.
Isaiah 14:3 KJV

Return unto thy rest, O my soul;
for the Lord hath dealt bountifully with thee.
Psalm 116:7 KJV

In quietness and in confidence shall be your strength.
Isaiah 30:15 KJV

Finally, brothers, rejoice. Be restored, be encouraged,
be of the same mind, be at peace,
and the God of love and peace will be with you.
2 Corinthians 13:11 HCSB

A Timely Tip

Working seven days a week may impress your boss, but it is not the way God intends for you to live your life. For further instructions, consult the Manual.

86

RIGHTEOUSNESS

The result of righteousness will be peace;
the effect of righteousness will be quiet confidence forever.
ISAIAH 32:17 HCSB

Every life, including yours, is a series of choices. Each day, you make countless decisions that will bring you closer to God, or not. The Lord wants you to live a holy life, a life that reflects an understanding of His Word and a love for His Son.

If we seek God's peace and His blessings, we must respect His teachings and obey them. When we're faced with a difficult choice or a powerful temptation, we should seek God's counsel and trust the counsel He gives.

The holy Bible contains careful instructions that, if followed, lead to fulfillment and salvation. But, if we choose to ignore God's commandments, the results are as predictable as they are tragic. So if you'd like a simple, surefire formula for abundant living, here it is: live righteously. And for further instructions, read the Manual.

*Becoming pure is a process of spiritual growth,
and taking seriously the confession of sin during prayer
time moves that process along, causing us to purge
our life of practices that displease God.*
ELIZABETH GEORGE

*Holiness has never been the driving force
of the majority. It is, however, mandatory for anyone
who wants to enter the kingdom.*
ELISABETH ELLIOT

*He doesn't need an abundance of words.
He doesn't need a dissertation about your life.
He just wants your attention. He wants your heart.*
KATHY TROCCOLI

*I believe the reason so many are failing today
is that they have not disciplined themselves
to read God's Word consistently, day in and day out,
and to apply it to every situation in life.*
KAY ARTHUR

*We have a decision to make—
to turn away from sin or to be miserable
and suffer the consequences of continual disobedience.*
VONETTE BRIGHT

More from God's Word

Discipline yourself for the purpose of godliness.
1 Timothy 4:7 NASB

But godliness with contentment is a great gain.
1 Timothy 6:6 HCSB

And let us not grow weary while doing good,
for in due season we shall reap if we do not lose heart.
Galatians 6:9 NKJV

Now by this we know that we know Him,
if we keep His commandments.
1 John 2:3 NKJV

For the eyes of the Lord are over the righteous,
and his ears are open unto their prayers:
but the face of the Lord is against them that do evil.
1 Peter 3:12 KJV

A Timely Tip

If you really want to follow Jesus, you must walk as He walked—you must strive to lead a righteous life, despite your imperfections. When you strive to please God with your thoughts, prayers, and deeds, you'll be eternally rewarded.

87
SERVICE

The greatest among you must be a servant.
But those who exalt themselves will be humbled,
and those who humble themselves will be exalted.
MATTHEW 23:11–12 NLT

Jesus teaches that the most esteemed men and women are not the leaders of society or the captains of industry. To the contrary, Jesus teaches that the greatest among us are those who choose to minister and to serve.

If you genuinely seek to discover God's unfolding purpose for your life, you must ask yourself this question: "How does God want me to serve?"

Whatever your path, whatever your calling, you may be certain of this: service to others is an integral part of God's plan for you. Christ was the ultimate servant, the Savior who gave His life for mankind. If we are to follow Him, we, too, must become humble servants.

Every single day of your life, including this one, God will give you opportunities to serve Him by serving His children. Welcome those opportunities with open arms. They are God's gift to you, His way of allowing you to achieve greatness in His kingdom.

God wants us to serve Him with a willing spirit,
one that would choose no other way.
BETH MOORE

In the very place where God has put us,
whatever its limitations, whatever kind of work it may be,
we may indeed serve the Lord Christ.
ELISABETH ELLIOT

Through our service to others,
God wants to influence our world for Him.
VONETTE BRIGHT

So many times we say that we can't serve God
because we aren't whatever is needed.
We're not talented enough or smart enough or whatever.
But if you are in covenant with Jesus Christ,
He is responsible for covering your weaknesses,
for being your strength. He will give you
His abilities for your disabilities!
KAY ARTHUR

God wants us to serve Him with a willing spirit,
one that would choose no other way.
BETH MOORE

More from God's Word

Shepherd God's flock, for whom you are responsible.
Watch over them because you want to,
not because you are forced. That is how God wants it.
Do it because you are happy to serve.
1 PETER 5:2 NCV

Blessed are those servants, whom the lord
when he cometh shall find watching.
LUKE 12:37 KJV

As each one has received a gift, minister it to one another,
as good stewards of the manifold grace of God.
1 PETER 4:10 NKJV

Assuredly, I say to you, inasmuch as you did it to one
of the least of these My brethren, you did it to Me.
MATTHEW 25:40 NKJV

Even so faith, if it hath not works, is dead, being alone.
JAMES 2:17 KJV

A Timely Tip

God wants you to serve Him now, not later. So, don't put off until tomorrow the good works you can perform for Him today.

88

SPEECH

A word fitly spoken is like apples of gold in settings of silver.
PROVERBS 25:11 NKJV

How much value do you place on the words you speak? Hopefully you understand that your words have great power . . . because they most certainly do. If your words are encouraging, you can lift others up; if your words are hurtful, you can hold others back.

When you're frustrated or tired, you may say things that would be better left unspoken. Whenever you lash out in anger, you forego the wonderful opportunity to consider your thoughts before you give voice to them. When you speak impulsively, you may, quite unintentionally, injure others.

A far better strategy, of course, is to do the more difficult thing: to think first and to speak next. When you do so, you give yourself ample time to compose your thoughts and to consult your Creator (but not necessarily in that order!).

Do you seek to be a source of encouragement to others? Are you a beacon of hope to your friends and family? And, do you seek to be a worthy ambassador for Christ? If so, you must speak words that are worthy of your Savior. So avoid angry outbursts. Refrain from impulsive outpourings. Terminate tantrums. Instead, speak words of encouragement and hope to a world that desperately needs both.

Watch your words diligently.
Words have such great power to bless or to wound.
When you speak carelessly or negatively,
you damage others as well as yourself.
SARAH YOUNG

A single word, if spoken in a friendly spirit,
may be sufficient to turn one from dangerous error.
FANNY CROSBY

We will always experience regret
when we live for the moment and do not weigh
our words and deeds before we give them life.
LISA BEVERE

The things that we feel most deeply
we ought to learn to be silent about,
at least until we have talked them over thoroughly with God.
ELISABETH ELLIOT

When you talk, choose the very same words
that you would use if Jesus were
looking over your shoulder. Because He is.
MARIE T. FREEMAN

More from God's Word

The heart of the wise teaches his mouth,
and adds learning to his lips.
PROVERBS 16:23 NKJV

If anyone thinks he is religious without controlling his tongue,
then his religion is useless and he deceives himself.
JAMES 1:26 HCSB

Pleasant words are a honeycomb:
sweet to the taste and health to the body.
PROVERBS 16:24 HCSB

What you have said in the dark will be heard in the light,
and what you have whispered in an inner room
will be shouted from the housetops.
LUKE 12:3 NCV

But encourage each other daily, while it is still called today,
so that none of you is hardened by sin's deception.
HEBREWS 3:13 HCSB

A Timely Tip

You can guard your heart by paying careful attention to the words you speak. Encouraging words have a way of encouraging everybody, and that includes you. So measure your words carefully and prayerfully.

89

SPIRITUAL GROWTH

I remind you to fan into flames the spiritual gift God gave you.
2 TIMOTHY 1:6 NLT

As a Christian, you should never stop growing. No matter your age, no matter your circumstances, you have opportunities to learn and opportunities to serve. Wherever you happen to be, God is there, too, and He wants to bless you with an expanding array of spiritual gifts. Your job is to let Him.

The path to spiritual maturity unfolds day by day. Through prayer, through Bible study, through silence, and through humble obedience to God's Word, we can strengthen our relationship with Him. The more we focus on the Father, the more He blesses our lives. The more carefully we listen for His voice, the more He teaches us.

In the quiet moments when we open our hearts to the Lord, the Creator who made us keeps remaking us. He gives us guidance, perspective, courage, and strength. And the appropriate moment to accept these spiritual gifts is always the present one.

God will help us become the people we are meant to be,
if only we will ask Him.
HANNAH WHITALL SMITH

Grow, dear friends, but grow, I beseech you,
in God's way, which is the only true way.
HANNAH WHITALL SMITH

We set our eyes on the finish line,
forgetting the past, and straining toward
the mark of spiritual maturity and fruitfulness.
VONETTE BRIGHT

Growing up in Christ is surely the most difficult,
courageous, exhilarating,
and eternally important work any of us will ever do.
SUSAN LENZKES

You are either becoming more like Christ
every day or you're becoming less like Him.
There is no neutral position in the Lord.
STORMIE OMARTIAN

More from God's Word

But endurance must do its complete work,
so that you may be mature and complete, lacking nothing.
JAMES 1:4 HCSB

And be not conformed to this world: but be ye transformed
by the renewing of your mind, that ye may prove what is that
good, and acceptable, and perfect, will of God.
ROMANS 12:2 KJV

But grow in the grace and knowledge of our Lord and Savior
Jesus Christ. To Him be the glory both now and forever. Amen.
2 PETER 3:18 NKJV

Leave inexperience behind, and you will live;
pursue the way of understanding.
PROVERBS 9:6 HCSB

So let us stop going over the basics of Christianity
again and again. Let us go on instead
and become mature in our understanding.
HEBREWS 6:1 NLT

A Timely Tip

When it comes to your faith, God doesn't want you to stand still. He wants you to keep growing. He knows that spiritual maturity is a journey, not a destination. You should know it, too.

90

STRENGTH

He gives strength to the weary,
and to him who lacks might He increases power.
ISAIAH 40:29 NASB

When you're weary or worried, where do you turn for strength? The medicine cabinet? The gym? The health food store? The spa? These places may offer a temporary energy boost, but the best place to turn for strength and solace isn't down the hall or at the mall; it's as near as your next breath. The best source of strength is God.

God's love for you never changes, and neither does His support. From the cradle to the grave, He has promised to give you the strength to meet the challenges of life. He has promised to guide you and protect you if you let Him. But He also expects you to do your part.

Today provides yet another opportunity to partake in the strength that only God can provide. You do so by attuning your heart to Him through prayer, obedience, and trust. Life can be challenging, but fear not. Whatever your challenge, God can give you the strength to face it and overcome it. Let Him.

*Nothing on earth compares to the strength God is willing
to interject into lives caught in the act of believing.*
BETH MOORE

*God will never lead you where
His strength cannot keep you.*
BARBARA JOHNSON

*Faith is a strong power,
mastering any difficulty in the strength
of the Lord who made heaven and earth.*
CORRIE TEN BOOM

*Are you weak? Weary? Confused? Troubled?
Pressured? How is your relationship with God?
Is it held in its place of priority? I believe
the greater the pressure, the greater
your need for time alone with Him.*
KAY ARTHUR

*When the dream of our heart is one that
God has planted there, a strange happiness
flows into us. At that moment, the spiritual resources
of the universe are released to help us.*
CATHERINE MARSHALL

More from God's Word

The LORD is my strength and my song;
He has become my salvation.
EXODUS 15:2 HCSB

Have faith in the LORD your God, and you will stand strong.
Have faith in his prophets, and you will succeed.
2 CHRONICLES 20:20 NCV

My grace is sufficient for you,
for my power is made perfect in weakness.
2 CORINTHIANS 12:9 NIV

Be strong and courageous, and do the work.
Don't be afraid or discouraged, for the LORD God, my God,
is with you. He won't leave you or forsake you.
1 CHRONICLES 28:20 HCSB

I can do all things through Christ who strengthens me.
PHILIPPIANS 4:13 NKJV

A Timely Tip

Need strength? Slow down, get more rest, engage in regular, sensible exercise, and turn your troubles over to God . . . but not necessarily in that order.

91

TEMPTATION

Your adversary, the devil,
prowls around like a roaring lion,
seeking someone to devour.
1 PETER 5:8 NASB

This world can be a dangerous place: enticements are everywhere. Even if you think you're in a very safe place today, be careful. Whether you realize it or not, your adversary is near, waiting for an opening, ready to strike you down if you drop your guard. The enemy has no pity, no compassion, no remorse. And, because he's far stronger than you, he'll eventually destroy you if you try to fight him singlehandedly.

You live in a society that is brimming with temptations and distractions. Never before in the entire history of humankind have adults and children alike been offered access to so many spiritual snares. Never before has the devil had so many tools.

So beware. Take a stand against your enemy. And ask for God's protection. Because your adversary never takes a day off. And neither should you.

Because Christ has faced our every temptation
without sin, we never face a temptation
that has no door of escape.
BETH MOORE

Temptation is not a sin. Even Jesus was tempted.
The Lord Jesus gives you the strength
needed to resist temptation.
CORRIE TEN BOOM

Flee temptation without leaving
a forwarding address.
BARBARA JOHNSON

The devil's most devilish when respectable.
ELIZABETH BARRETT BROWNING

The first step on the way to victory
is to recognize the enemy.
CORRIE TEN BOOM

More from God's Word

*No temptation has overtaken you but such as is common
to man; and God is faithful, who will not allow you
to be tempted beyond what you are able, but with
the temptation will provide the way of escape.*
1 Corinthians 10:13 NASB

*Put on the whole armor of God, that you may
be able to stand against the wiles of the devil.*
Ephesians 6:11 NKJV

Do not be misled: "Bad company corrupts good character."
1 Corinthians 15:33 NIV

*But encourage each other daily, while it is still called today,
so that none of you is hardened by sin's deception.*
Hebrews 3:13 HCSB

*Let us lay aside every weight, and the sin
which so easily ensnares us, and let us run
with endurance the race that is set before us.*
Hebrews 12:1 NKJV

A Timely Tip

Every day of your life, you will be tempted to rebel against God's teachings. Your job, simply put, is to guard your heart against the darkness as you focus on the light.

92

THANKSGIVING

Enter into His gates with thanksgiving,
and into His courts with praise. Be thankful to Him,
and bless His name. For the LORD is good; His mercy
is everlasting, and His truth endures to all generations.
PSALM 100:4–5 NKJV

When we consider God's blessings and the sacrifices of His Son, just how thankful should we be? Should we praise our Creator once a day? Are two prayers enough? Is it sufficient that we thank our heavenly Father at mealtimes and bedtimes? The answer, of course, is no. When we consider how richly we have been blessed, now and forever—and when we consider the price Christ paid on the cross—it becomes clear that we should offer many prayers of thanks throughout the day. But all too often, amid the hustle of daily life, we forget to pause and praise the Giver of all good gifts.

Our lives expand or contract in proportion to our gratitude. When we are appropriately grateful for God's countless blessings, we experience His peace. But if we ignore His gifts, we invite stress, anxiety, and sadness into our lives.

Throughout this day, pause and say silent prayers of thanks. When you do, you'll discover that a grateful heart reaps countless blessings that a hardened heart will never know.

*God is worthy of our praise and is pleased
when we come before Him with thanksgiving.*
SHIRLEY DOBSON

*Fill up the spare moments of your life
with praise and thanksgiving.*
SARAH YOUNG

*God is in control, and therefore in everything
I can give thanks—not because of the situation
but because of the One who directs and rules over it.*
KAY ARTHUR

*I have learned that in every circumstance
that comes my way, I can choose to respond
in one of two ways: I can whine or I can worship!
And I can't worship without giving thanks.
It just isn't possible.*
NANCY LEIGH DEMOSS

*The act of thanksgiving is a demonstration
of the fact that you are going to trust and believe God.*
KAY ARTHUR

More from God's Word

And whatever you do, in word or in deed,
do everything in the name of the Lord Jesus,
giving thanks to God the Father through Him.
Colossians 3:17 HCSB

Surely the righteous shall give thanks to Your name;
the upright shall dwell in Your presence.
Psalm 140:13 NKJV

Rejoice always, pray without ceasing, in everything give thanks;
for this is the will of God in Christ Jesus for you.
1 Thessalonians 5:16–18 NKJV

I will thank the Lord with all my heart;
I will declare all Your wonderful works. I will rejoice and boast
about You; I will sing about Your name, Most High.
Psalm 9:1–2 HCSB

Thanks be to God for His indescribable gift.
2 Corinthians 9:15 HCSB

A Timely Tip

Every sunrise represents yet another beautifully wrapped gift from God. Unwrap it; treasure it; use it; and give thanks to the Giver.

93

THOUGHTS

Set your mind on things above, not on things on the earth.
COLOSSIANS 3:2 NKJV

Because we are human, we are always busy with our thoughts. We simply can't help ourselves. Our brains never shut off, and even while we're sleeping, we mull things over in our minds. The question is not if we will think; the question is how we will think and what we will think about. And all too often, we allow the worries of everyday life to overwhelm our thoughts and cloud our vision. What's needed is clearer perspective, renewed faith, and a different focus.

When we focus on the frustrations of today or the uncertainties of tomorrow, we rob ourselves of peace in the present moment. But, when we direct our thoughts in more positive directions, we rob our worries of the power to tyrannize us.

American poet Phoebe Cary observed, "All the great blessings of my life are present in my thoughts today." And her words apply to you. You will make your life better when you focus your thoughts on your blessings, not your misfortunes. So do yourself, your family, your friends, and your coworkers a favor: Learn to think optimistically about the world you live in and the life you lead. Then, prepare yourself for the blessings that good thoughts will bring.

It is not so much adverse events
that make you anxious
as it is your thoughts about those events.
SARAH YOUNG

The things we think are the things that feed our souls.
If we think on pure and lovely things, we shall grow pure
and lovely like them; and the converse is equally true.
HANNAH WHITALL SMITH

Our actions, habits, character,
and future are most definitely
affected by our thoughts.
ELIZABETH GEORGE

Remember, you become what you think.
Think discouraging thoughts,
and you'll get discouraged.
JOYCE MEYER

We can't really tell how crooked
our thinking is until we line it up
with the straight edge of Scripture.
ELISABETH ELLIOT

More from God's Word

The peace of God, which surpasses all understanding,
will guard your hearts and minds through Christ Jesus.
PHILIPPIANS 4:7 NKJV

Guard your heart above all else, for it is the source of life.
PROVERBS 4:23 HCSB

Finally, brothers, whatever is true, whatever is noble,
whatever is right, whatever is pure, whatever is lovely,
whatever is admirable—if anything is excellent
or praiseworthy—think about such things.
PHILIPPIANS 4:8 NIV

And do not be conformed to this world, but be transformed
by the renewing of your mind, so that you may prove what
the will of God is, that which is good and acceptable and perfect.
ROMANS 12:2 NASB

For to be carnally minded is death,
but to be spiritually minded is life and peace.
ROMANS 8:6 NKJV

A Timely Tip

Unless you're willing to guard your thoughts, you'll never be able to guard your heart. So focus on blessings, not hardships, and opportunities, not roadblocks.

94
TODAY

This is the day the Lord has made;
let us rejoice and be glad in it.
PSALM 118:24 HCSB

All the days on the calendar have one thing in common: They're all gifts from God. So this day, like every day, is a cause for celebration as we consider God's blessings and His love.

How will you invest this day? Will you treat your time as a commodity too precious to be squandered? Will you carve out time during the day to serve God by serving His children? Will you celebrate God's gifts and obey His commandments? And will you share words of encouragement with the people who cross your path? The answers to these questions will determine, to a surprising extent, the quality of your day and the quality of your life.

So, wherever you find yourself today, take time to celebrate and give thanks for another priceless gift from the Father. The present moment is precious. Treat it that way.

When your life comes to a close,
you will remember not days but moments.
Treasure each one.

BARBARA JOHNSON

Commitment to His lordship on Easter,
at revivals, or even every Sunday is not enough.
We must choose this day—and every day—whom we will serve.
This deliberate act of the will is the inevitable choice between
habitual fellowship and habitual failure.

BETH MOORE

Every day we live is a priceless gift of God,
loaded with possibilities to learn something new,
to gain fresh insights.

DALE EVANS ROGERS

Today is mine. Tomorrow is none of my business.
If I peer anxiously into the fog of the future,
I will strain my spiritual eyes so that I will not see clearly
what is required of me now.

ELISABETH ELLIOT

Submit each day to God,
knowing that He is God over all your tomorrows.

KAY ARTHUR

More from God's Word

But encourage each other every day while it is "today."
Help each other so none of you will become
hardened because sin has tricked you.
HEBREWS 3:13 NCV

There is a time for everything,
and a season for every activity under heavens.
ECCLESIASTES 3:1 NIV

So don't worry about tomorrow, because tomorrow will have its
own worries. Each day has enough trouble of its own.
MATTHEW 6:34 NCV

The world and its desires pass away,
but the man who does the will of God lives forever.
1 JOHN 2:17 NIV

So teach us to number our days,
that we may present to You a heart of wisdom.
PSALM 90:12 NASB

A Timely Tip

Today is a wonderful, one-of-a-kind gift from God. Treat it that way.

95

TRUSTING GOD

Trust in the LORD with all your heart,
and lean not on your own understanding;
in all your ways acknowledge Him,
and He shall direct your paths.

PROVERBS 3:5–6 NKJV

Sometimes the future seems bright, and sometimes it does not. Yet even when we cannot see the possibilities of tomorrow, God can. As believers, our challenge is to trust an uncertain future to an all-powerful God.

When we trust God, we should trust Him without reservation. We should steel ourselves against the inevitable disappointments of the day, secure in the knowledge that our heavenly Father has a plan for the future that only He can see.

Can you place your future into the hands of a loving and all-knowing God? Can you live amid the uncertainties of today, knowing that God has dominion over all your tomorrows? If you can, you are wise and you are blessed. When you trust God with everything you are and everything you have, He will bless you now and forever.

Trust God's Word and His power more than
you trust your own feelings and experiences.
Remember, your Rock is Christ, and it is the sea
that ebbs and flows with the tides, not Him.
LETTIE COWMAN

Never be afraid to trust an unknown future to a known God.
CORRIE TEN BOOM

Sometimes the very essence of faith
is trusting God in the midst of things
He knows good and well we cannot comprehend.
BETH MOORE

Are you serious about wanting God's guidance
to become the person He wants you to be?
The first step is to tell God that you know you
can't manage your own life; that you need His help.
CATHERINE MARSHALL

Do not be afraid, then, that if you trust,
or tell others to trust, the matter will end there.
Trust is only the beginning and the continual foundation.
When we trust Him, the Lord works, and His work
is the important part of the whole matter.
HANNAH WHITALL SMITH

MORE FROM GOD'S WORD

In quietness and trust is your strength.
ISAIAH 30:15 NASB

The fear of man is a snare,
but the one who trusts in the LORD is protected.
PROVERBS 29:25 HCSB

The LORD is my rock, my fortress, and my deliverer,
my God, my mountain where I seek refuge. My shield, the horn
of my salvation, my stronghold, my refuge, and my Savior.
2 SAMUEL 22:2–3 HCSB

Those who trust in the LORD are like Mount Zion.
It cannot be shaken; it remains forever.
PSALM 125:1 HCSB

Jesus said, "Don't let your hearts be troubled.
Trust in God, and trust in me."
JOHN 14:1 NCV

A TIMELY TIP

Because God is trustworthy—and because He has made promises to you that He intends to keep—you are protected. The Lord always keeps His promises. Trust Him.

96
TRUTH

You will know the truth, and the truth will set you free.
JOHN 8:32 HCSB

God is vitally concerned with truth. His Word teaches the truth; His Spirit reveals the truth; His Son leads us to the truth. When we open our hearts to God, and when we allow His Son to rule over our thoughts and our lives, God reveals Himself, and we come to understand the truth about ourselves and the Truth (with a capital T) about God's gift of grace.

The familiar words of John 8:32 remind us that when we come to know God's Truth, we are liberated. Have you been liberated by that Truth? And are you living in accordance with the eternal truths that you find in God's holy Word? Hopefully so.

Today, as you fulfill the responsibilities that God has placed before you, ask yourself this question: "Do my thoughts and actions bear witness to the ultimate Truth that God has placed in my heart, or am I allowing the pressures of everyday life to overwhelm me?" It's a profound question that deserves an answer now.

Those who walk in truth walk in liberty.
BETH MOORE

We are either in the process of resisting God's truth or in the process of being shaped and molded by His truth.
MARY C. NEAL

God will see to it that we understand as much truth as we are willing to obey.
ELISABETH ELLIOT

The Holy Spirit was given to guide us into all truth, but He doesn't do it all at once.
ELISABETH ELLIOT

While walking through a dark season, if we attempt to navigate our lives by what we feel, we will run aground onto the rocks. We must navigate by what we know is true no matter what we feel.
SHEILA WALSH

More from God's Word

When the Spirit of truth comes,
He will guide you into all the truth.
JOHN 16:13 HCSB

But do not follow foolish stories that disagree
with God's truth, but train yourself to serve God.
1 TIMOTHY 4:7 NCV

Jesus said, "I am the Road, also the Truth,
also the Life. No one gets to the Father apart from me."
JOHN 14:6 MSG

Learn the truth and never reject it.
Get wisdom, self-control, and understanding.
PROVERBS 23:23 NCV

Teach me Your way, O LORD;
I will walk in Your truth.
PSALM 86:11 NASB

A Timely Tip

Jesus offers you the Truth with a capital T. How you respond to His Truth will determine the direction—and the destination—of your life.

97

WISDOM

The fear of the LORD is the beginning of knowledge,
but fools despise wisdom and instruction.
PROVERBS 1:7 NKJV

All the wisdom that you'll ever need to live a meaningful life can be found in a single book: the Bible. God's Word guides us along a path that leads to abundance and eternal life. When we embrace Biblical teachings and follow God's Son, we're protected. But, when we wander from His path, we inevitably suffer the consequences of our mistaken priorities.

In theory, all of us would prefer to be wise, but not all of us are willing to make the sacrifices that are required to gain real wisdom. To become wise, we must do more than spout platitudes, recite verses, or repeat aphorisms. We must not only speak wisely; we must live wisely. We must not only learn the lessons of the Christian life; we must live by them.

Today, as you think about the best way to live and the best way to lead, remember that God's wisdom can be found in a book that's already on your bookshelf: His Book. Read, heed, and live accordingly.

*If we neglect the Bible, we cannot expect
to benefit from the wisdom and direction
that result from knowing God's Word.*
VONETTE BRIGHT

*Knowledge can be found in books or in school.
Wisdom, on the other hand,
starts with God . . . and ends there.*
MARIE T. FREEMAN

*Wisdom is the God-given ability to see life
with rare objectivity and to handle life with rare stability.*
ELIZABETH GEORGE

*Wisdom is knowledge applied.
Head knowledge is useless on the battlefield.
Knowledge stamped on the heart makes one wise.*
BETH MOORE

*When you and I are related to Jesus Christ,
our strength and wisdom and peace and joy
and love and hope may run out, but His life rushes in
to keep us filled to the brim. We are showered with blessings,
not because of anything we have or have not done,
but simply because of Him.*
ANNE GRAHAM LOTZ

More from God's Word

Acquire wisdom—how much better it is than gold!
And acquire understanding—it is preferable to silver.
PROVERBS 16:16 HCSB

He that walketh with wise men shall be wise:
but a companion of fools shall be destroyed.
PROVERBS 13:20 KJV

But the wisdom that is from above is first pure,
then peaceable, gentle, willing to yield, full of mercy
and good fruits, without partiality and without hypocrisy.
JAMES 3:17 NKJV

But if any of you lacks wisdom, let him ask of God,
who gives to all generously and without reproach,
and it will be given to him.
JAMES 1:5 NASB

Who among you is wise and understanding? Let him show
by his good behavior his deeds in the gentleness of wisdom.
JAMES 3:13 NASB

A Timely Tip

Wisdom begins with a thorough understanding of God's moral order, the eternal truths that are found in His holy Word. Real wisdom is more than mere knowledge. It's the application of God's truth in everyday life.

98
WORK

*Whatever you do, do it enthusiastically,
as something done for the Lord and not for men.*
COLOSSIANS 3:23 HCSB

The old saying is both familiar and true: We should pray as if everything depended upon the Lord but work as if everything depended upon us. Yet sometimes, when we are tired or discouraged, our worries can sap our strength and sidetrack our motivation. But God has other intentions. He expects us to work for the things that we pray for. More importantly, God intends that our work become His work.

As you seek to accomplish your goals and fulfill God's plan for your life, your success will depend, in large part, upon the passion that you bring to your work. God has created a world in which hard work is rewarded and laziness is not. So don't look for short-cuts (because there aren't any) and don't expect easy solutions to life's biggest challenges (because big rewards usually require lots of effort). You inhabit a world in which instant gratification is rare, but the rewards of hard work are not. Shape your expectations—and your work habits—accordingly.

Are you desiring some spiritual blessing?
Then dig the ditches and God will fill them.
But He will do this in the most unexpected places
and in the most unexpected ways.

LETTIE COWMAN

What is needed for happy effectual service
is simply to put your work into the Lord's hand,
and leave it there.

HANNAH WHITALL SMITH

Ordinary work, which is what most of us do
most of the time, is ordained by God
every bit as much as is the extraordinary.

ELISABETH ELLIOT

You can't climb the ladder of life
with your hands in your pockets.

BARBARA JOHNSON

Great relief and satisfaction can come from seeking God's
priorities for us in each season, discerning what is "best" in
the midst of many noble opportunities, and pouring our most
excellent energies into those things.

BETH MOORE

More from God's Word

*But this I say: He who sows sparingly will also reap sparingly,
and he who sows bountifully will also reap bountifully.*
2 Corinthians 9:6 NKJV

*The plans of hard-working people earn a profit,
but those who act too quickly become poor.*
Proverbs 21:5 NCV

*Be strong and courageous, and do the work.
Don't be afraid or discouraged, for the Lord God,
my God, is with you. He won't leave you or forsake you.*
1 Chronicles 28:20 HCSB

*Do you see a man skilled in his work?
He will stand in the presence of kings.*
Proverbs 22:29 HCSB

*I must work the works of Him who sent Me while it is day;
the night is coming when no one can work.*
John 9:4 NKJV

A Timely Tip

Here's a time-tested formula for success: have faith in God and
do the work. Hard work is not simply a proven way to get ahead, it's
also part of God's plan for all His children (including you).

99

WORRY

Therefore do not worry about tomorrow,
for tomorrow will worry about its own things.
Sufficient for the day is its own trouble.

MATTHEW 6:34 NKJV

Because we are fallible human beings struggling through the inevitable challenges of life here on earth, we worry. Even though we, as Christians, have been promised the gift of eternal life—even though we, as Christians, are blessed by God's love and protection—we find ourselves fretting over the inevitable frustrations of everyday life.

Where is the best place to take your worries? Take them to God. Take your concerns to Him; take your fears to Him; take your doubts to Him; take your weaknesses to Him; take your sorrows to Him . . . and leave them all there. Seek protection from the Creator and build your spiritual house upon the Rock that cannot be moved. Remember that God still sits in His heaven and you are His beloved child. Then, perhaps, you will worry less and trust Him more. And that's as it should be because the Lord is trustworthy . . .and you are protected.

Worries carry responsibilities that belong to God,
not to you. Worry does not enable us to escape evil;
it makes us unfit to cope with it when it comes.

CORRIE TEN BOOM

Do not hide from your fear or pretend that it isn't there.
Anxiety that you hide in the recesses of your heart will give
birth to fear of fear.

SARAH YOUNG

Replace worry with prayer. Make the decision
to pray whenever you catch yourself worrying.

ELIZABETH GEORGE

Worries, if indulged, develop into idols.
Anxiety gains a life of its own,
parasitically infesting your mind.

SARAH YOUNG

Worry is like a rocking chair.
It keeps you moving but doesn't get you anywhere.

CORRIE TEN BOOM

More from God's Word

Let not your heart be troubled;
you believe in God, believe also in Me.
JOHN 14:1 NKJV

Peace I leave with you; My peace I give to you;
not as the world gives do I give to you.
Do not let your heart be troubled, nor let it be fearful.
JOHN 14:27 NASB

Cast all your anxiety on him because he cares for you.
1 PETER 5:7 NIV

Do not be anxious about anything, but in everything,
by prayer and petition, with thanksgiving,
present your requests to God.
PHILIPPIANS 4:6 NIV

Cast your burden on the LORD, and He shall sustain you;
He shall never permit the righteous to be moved.
PSALM 55:22 NKJV

A Timely Tip

God always keeps His promises. Remembering His faithfulness in the past can give you peace for today and hope for tomorrow. So, turn your worries over to God. He can handle them. And He will.

100

WORSHIP

I was glad when they said unto me,
Let us go into the house of the LORD.
PSALM 122:1 KJV

To worship God is a privilege, but it's a privilege that far too many of us forego. Instead of praising our Creator seven days a week, we worship on Sunday mornings (if at all) and spend the rest of the week focusing on other things.

Whenever we become distracted by worldly pursuits that put God in second place, we inevitably pay the price of our misplaced priorities. A better strategy, of course, is to worship Him every day of the week, beginning with a regular early-morning devotional.

Every new day provides another opportunity to worship God with grateful hearts and helping hands. And, each day offers another chance to support the church He created. When we do, we bless others—and we are blessed by the One who sent His only begotten Son so that we might have eternal life.

We worship in Thy holy Name;
O! bless this hour of prayer.
FANNY CROSBY

Even the most routine part of your day
can be a spiritual act of worship.
SARAH YOUNG

Worship is focus.
BETH MOORE

Worship is an inward reverence,
the bowing down of the soul in the presence of God.
ELIZABETH GEORGE

Two wings are necessary to lift our souls toward God:
prayer and praise. Prayer asks.
Praise accepts the answer.
LETTIE COWMAN

More from God's Word

*Happy are those who hear the joyful call to worship,
for they will walk in the light of your presence, LORD.*
PSALM 89:15 NLT

*God is Spirit, and those who worship Him
must worship in spirit and truth.*
JOHN 4:24 HCSB

*All the earth will worship You and sing praise to You.
They will sing praise to Your name.*
PSALM 66:4 HCSB

*For where two or three are gathered together in My name,
I am there among them.*
MATTHEW 18:20 HCSB

*Worship the LORD with gladness. Come before him,
singing with joy. Acknowledge that the LORD is God! He made
us, and we are his. We are his people, the sheep of his pasture.*
PSALM 100:2–3 NLT

A Timely Tip

Worship is not meant to be confined to a church building on Sunday morning. Praise and worship should be woven into the very fabric of our lives. It always pays to always praise.

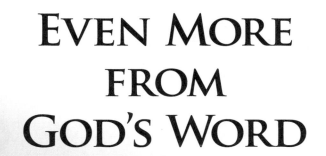

Even More From God's Word

More from God's Word
About Assurance

This is the secret: Christ lives in you.
This gives you assurance of sharing his glory
COLOSSIANS 1:27 NLT

Let us draw near with a true heart in full assurance of faith,
our hearts sprinkled clean from an evil conscience
and our bodies washed in pure water.
HEBREWS 10:22 HCSB

As for God, his way is perfect: the word of the LORD is tried:
he is a buckler to all those that trust in him.
PSALM 18:30 KJV

In quietness and in confidence shall be your strength.
ISAIAH 30:15 KJV

Let us hold tightly without wavering to the hope we affirm,
for God can be trusted to keep his promise.
HEBREWS 10:23 NLT

For our gospel came not unto you in word only, but also in
power, and in the Holy Ghost, and in much assurance.
1 THESSALONIANS 1:5 KJV

More from God's Word About Behavior

Now by this we know that we know Him,
if we keep His commandments.
1 John 2:3 NKJV

Walk in a manner worthy of the God
who calls you into His own kingdom and glory.
1 Thessalonians 2:12 NASB

Live peaceful and quiet lives
in all godliness and holiness.
1 Timothy 2:2 NIV

But prove yourselves doers of the word,
and not merely hearers who delude themselves.
James 1:22 NASB

To do evil is like sport to a fool,
but a man of understanding has wisdom.
Proverbs 10:23 NKJV

In everything set them an example by doing what is good.
Titus 2:7 NIV

More from God's Word About Change

To every thing there is a season,
and a time to every purpose under the heaven.
ECCLESIASTES 3:1 KJV

The wise see danger ahead and avoid it,
but fools keep going and get into trouble.
PROVERBS 22:3 NCV

But grow in the grace and knowledge
of our Lord and Savior Jesus Christ.
To Him be the glory both now and forever. Amen.
2 PETER 3:18 NKJV

When I was a child, I spoke like a child,
I thought like a child, I reasoned like a child.
When I became a man, I put aside childish things.
1 CORINTHIANS 13:11 HCSB

Then He who sat on the throne said,
"Behold, I make all things new."
REVELATION 21:5 NKJV

I am the LORD, and I do not change.
MALACHI 3:6 NLT

More from God's Word About Choices

If you need wisdom,
ask our generous God, and he will give it to you.
He will not rebuke you for asking.
JAMES 1:5 NLT

Who is wise and has understanding among you? He should
show his works by good conduct with wisdom's gentleness.
JAMES 3:13 HCSB

The fear of the LORD is the beginning of knowledge,
but fools despise wisdom and discipline.
PROVERBS 1:7 NIV

A good man produces good out of the good storeroom of his
heart, and an evil man produces evil out of the evil storeroom,
for his mouth speaks from the overflow of the heart.
LUKE 6:45 HCSB

Blessed is the man who walks not in the counsel
of the ungodly, nor stands in the path of sinners,
nor sits in the seat of the scornful.
PSALM 1:1 NKJV

More from God's Word About Duty

I must work the works of him that sent me, while it is day:
the night cometh, when no man can work.
John 9:4 KJV

And we desire that each one of you show the same diligence
so as to realize the full assurance of hope until the end,
so that you will not be sluggish, but imitators of those who
through faith and patience inherit the promises.
Hebrews 6:11–12 NASB

Be strong and courageous, and do the work.
Don't be afraid or discouraged, for the Lord God,
my God, is with you. He won't leave you or forsake you.
1 Chronicles 28:20 HCSB

So then each of us shall give account of himself to God.
Romans 14:12 NKJV

I am He who searches the minds and hearts;
and I will give to each one of you according to your deeds.
Revelation 2:23 NASB

Here now is my final conclusion: Fear God
and obey his commands, for this is everyone's duty.
Ecclesiastes 12:13 NLT

More from God's Word About Envy

Let us not be desirous of vainglory,
provoking one another, envying one another.
GALATIANS 5:26 KJV

So rid yourselves of all wickedness, all deceit,
hypocrisy, envy, and all slander.
1 PETER 2:1 HCSB

You must not covet your neighbor's house. You must not covet
your neighbor's wife, male or female servant, ox or donkey,
or anything else that belongs to your neighbor.
EXODUS 20:17 NLT

Let us not become boastful, challenging one another,
envying one another.
GALATIANS 5:26 NASB

Where jealousy and selfishness are,
there will be confusion and every kind of evil.
JAMES 3:16 NCV

Don't envy evil men or desire to be with them.
PROVERBS 24:1 HCSB

More from God's Word About Grace

*But because of his great love for us, God, who is rich
in mercy, made us alive with Christ even when we were dead
in transgressions—it is by grace you have been saved.*
EPHESIANS 2:4–5 NIV

*But grow in the grace and knowledge of
our Lord and Savior Jesus Christ. To Him be the glory,
both now and to the day of eternity.*
2 PETER 3:18 NASB

*In Him we have redemption through His blood,
the forgiveness of our trespasses,
according to the riches of His grace
that He lavished on us with all wisdom and understanding.*
EPHESIANS 1:7–8 HCSB

*My grace is sufficient for you,
for my power is made perfect in weakness.*
2 CORINTHIANS 12:9 NIV

*But he gives us more grace. That is why Scripture says:
"God opposes the proud but gives grace to the humble."*
JAMES 4:6 NIV

MORE FROM GOD'S WORD ABOUT QUIET TIME

*Now in the morning, having risen a long while
before daylight, He went out and departed
to a solitary place; and there He prayed.*
MARK 1:35 NKJV

*Truly my soul silently waits for God;
from Him comes my salvation.*
PSALM 62:1 NKJV

Be still, and know that I am God.
PSALM 46:10 KJV

Listen in silence before me.
ISAIAH 41:1 NLT

*In quietness and in confidence
shall be your strength.*
ISAIAH 30:15 KJV

*To everything there is a season . . .
a time to keep silence, and a time to speak.*
ECCLESIASTES 3:1,7 KJV

More from God's Word About Success

*May he give you the desire of your heart
and make all your plans succeed.*
PSALM 20:4 NIV

*Trust in the Lord with all your heart,
and lean not on your own understanding; in all your
ways acknowledge Him, and He shall direct your paths.*
PROVERBS 3:5-6 NKJV

*There is no wisdom, understanding,
or advice that can succeed against the Lord.*
PROVERBS 21:30 NCV

*He who works his land will have abundant food,
but he who chases fantasies lacks judgment.*
PROVERBS 12:11 NIV

*All goes well for those who are generous,
who lend freely and conduct their business fairly.*
PSALMS 112:5 NLT

*Who are those who fear the Lord? He will show them
the path they should choose. They will live in prosperity,
and their children will inherit the Promised Land.*
PSALM 25:12-13 NLT

More from God's Word About Your Testimony

For God has not given us a spirit of fear and timidity,
but of power, love, and self-discipline.
So never be ashamed to tell others about our Lord.
2 Timothy 1:7–8 NLT

And I say to you, anyone who acknowledges
Me before men, the Son of Man will also acknowledge
him before the angels of God.
Luke 12:8 HCSB

You must worship Christ as Lord of your life.
And if someone asks about your hope as a believer,
always be ready to explain it.
1 Peter 3:15 NLT

All those who stand before others and say they believe in me,
I will say before my Father in heaven that they belong to me.
Matthew 10:32 NCV

When they had prayed, the place where they were assembled
was shaken, and they were all filled with the Holy Spirit
and began to speak God's message with boldness.
Acts 4:31 HCSB